CW01660573

Walking Aloud

Kim Taplin, author of *The English Path*, is a writer and poet whose work celebrates the earth and walking across it.

This book has its roots in a small rough diamond of Oxfordshire from Kidlington to Banbury and from Kirtlington to Stonesfield, and is centred on Tackley where she has lived for the last forty years.

But it also ranges more widely, conveying the inexhaustible interest and pleasure of exploring anywhere on foot, and the unique role of walking for savouring the life of a particular place and reflecting on our place in the natural world.

By the same author

The English Path
Tongues in Trees
Three Women in a Boat
Life with Art

Poetry

By the Harbour Wall
From Parched Creek
Snow Buntings at Barton Point
Goodfellow

WALKING ALOUD

RAMBLES IN THE CHERWELL VALLEY

KIM TAPLIN

With illustrations by Rachael Sherlaw-Johnson

THE WYCHWOOD PRESS

Acknowledgement

Permission to quote from *The Autobiography of a Supertramp* by W.H. Davies is kindly given by Kieron Griffin, trustee of the Mrs. H.M. Davies Will Trust.

First published in 2008 by
The Wychwood Press
an imprint of Jon Carpenter Publishing
Alder House, Market Street, Charlbury, Oxfordshire OX7 3PH

ISBN 978 1 902279 33 6

Our books may be ordered from bookshops or (post free) from
The Wychwood Press, Alder House, Market Street, Charlbury, OX7 3PH
01608 811969

e-mail: orders@wychwoodpress.co.uk

Credit card orders should be phoned or faxed to 01689 870437 or 01608 811969

All our books may be seen at www.wychwoodpress.co.uk

Printed and bound in Great Britain by Cpod, Trowbridge, Wiltshire

To Deborah, Jeanie, Monika, and Tess

PREAMBLE

In my late teens I went on a walking holiday with a boyfriend. Looking back, it seems a rather old-fashioned thing for us to have done — in my mind's eye we look like those healthy outdoor chaps and girls in socks and shorts and knapsacks on the covers of the old Ordnance Survey maps. But it probably was actually 1963, the year wherein Philip Larkin famously located the start of a whole new ball-game, and we wanted to share a room. We knocked on the door of a B&B for the first time and enquired, and the boyfriend, thinking to give us more gravitas but actually undermining it further, added, 'We're from the Amblers' Association'. I can remember them smiling a little, with amusement and tolerance, and then, I think, letting us in.

I have remained a life member of the Amblers. It suits my liking for uffish thought, for turning stones over to witness the strange life under them, for stopping to sniff at dog-roses. For digressing. Sometimes I've forgotten and let myself get caught up in the general conviction that we need to hurry because there are Places to Go and Things to Do, but eventually I've always returned to myself and remembered that I have something that for want of a better word I call a soul, and that it's thirsty.

It's an easy pace, the amble, and one that conduces to happiness — and to the proliferation of foot-notes. I am also a member of the Ramblers', because they work to guard our footpaths; and that rich common inheritance that isn't physical, the right to walk where we don't own, the access to so much that is interesting and beautiful, is what I want to celebrate.

To acknowledge where you found something that you've assimilated isn't always easy. We forget. The most potent influences quickly become part of ourselves and invisible to us. But any acknowledgement we can make is a small act to check the cold rise of individualism, to remind ourselves that as seeds we are nourished by the soil of culture. We don't always (or ever completely) understand what we are seeing and experiencing. But I've sometimes dreamed that if the usual order of things were to be reversed, if the footnotes were the main text, that it might encourage a greater gentleness. More sharing and less competition.

The settled and farmed English countryside, with what wild remains beneath or within it, and the footpaths that are ways in for all of us to enjoy it, also the friends and writers and artists who have helped open my eyes to it — these are the sources that nourish me. The world of nature is rich and untidy like the imagination, and where we can still get in touch with it we can rehydrate. Where it is too damaged or controlled we parch. This is what W.H. Davies, the Supertramp, wrote concerning the time when he set off walking into the English countryside:

> I lost for the time being my vision of the future, being filled with the peace of present objects. I noted with joy the first green field after the park, the first bird that differed from the sparrow, the first stile in the hedge … the first footpath across the wild common …'

The peace of present objects: says it all really.

As a child I had a fanciful idea — perhaps I read it somewhere — that angels constantly watched, not just human beings but everything, every bird and animal and bug, every tiny plant; and I thought that in some way, by observing (I owned a number of Observer Books) you were helping, taking a turn on watch as I'd heard sailors do. It seemed a delightful thing, and a privilege, thus to share the angels' work. I no longer believe in angels (more's the pity); but I still like the birders' epithet 'well-watched'. In describing a place as 'well-watched', they speak dryly of labours of love, shared information, increased understanding.

Also I'm out to meet the man in brown. There's a nursery rhyme that goes:

Dickery dickery dare
The pig flew up in the air
The man in brown
Soon brought him down
Dickery dickery dare

— a seemingly inconsequential jingle that has survived, its origins forgotten, when a thousand others perished. Researched, it may turn out that the pig was, say, some Prime Minister or other, and the Man in Brown perhaps his Chancellor of the Exchequer; and though no doubt it was considered, or in fact was, an excellent piece of wit at the time, it feels now like a disappointing reduction. More resonant — and could this be why it survived? — is what it suggests about the nature of things. Because maybe the collective imagination is a shrewd old luvvie holding auditions. He knows what he's looking for though he'd be hard put to define it — some quality having life in it, some aspect of potential rather than perfectedness. A spark, something that opens the mind's eye a little.

Next, he growls. *Next, next. Don't call us. Next.* And then suddenly it's there — something has hooked him although he thinks he's doing the hooking. Or maybe it's all just random ...

Whatever the truth, to me this rhyme says Archetype. Earthiest of creatures, once sacred and so, as our perverse way is, sacrificed (according to the venerable Brewer) to Ceres 'because it taught men to turn up the earth', *a pig has no business in the air.* Apart from looking ridiculous, it can't rootle and will soon starve. Does this ring any bells? I don't just mean inflated armchair theorists or the hippy when he mutters 'don't bring me down, man' or the devotees of ungrounded religions. I mean all of us, who as soon as we have the least little bit of wealth or power tend to take off, rise above the mud and float, bizarre, spirits unfed, in a fantasy of entitlement and security, ignoring what's happening on the ground, heedless of the cost to the earth of keeping us up there. Not just air travel. I mean the whole greedy stupid consumerist shebang.

So if we are the pigs, who or what is the man in brown, who sounds, in the rhyme, so competent and grounded? That comforting word 'soon' is like when the doctor says 'we'll soon have you back on your feet again'; or at least it's comforting if that's what you want. If not, the verse can have a punitive sound: the man in brown must be a puritan, a doom monger, a spoilsport. Admittedly, brown's not a fun colour. In the prismatic sense it's not really a colour at all; but it's the hue of home, the earth, of rot and soil, and night soil, and we can't live without it. So the man in brown can be a figure of the earth itself, of that which makes greenness possible, and poppies and kingfishers and corn, and the whole gorgeous teeming cornucopia.

The poets know him: he crops up everywhere in literature. He's Shakespeare's Puck, laughing at the follies of mortals and mischievously toppling them down to earth. Walt Whitman in his *Song of Myself* takes him as a persona: 'look for me under your bootsoles'. He's Pan in *The Wind in the Willows*; he's Edward Thomas's *Lob*. He's Gabriel Oak in *Far From the Madding Crowd*, whose expert surgery punctures the bloated flock and saves them. Tolkien's Tom Bombadil is brightly clad — the earth in all its glory — but we can recognise him at once when he doctors Frodo's inflation and is the only character over whom the ring of power is powerless.

What I get from my ambling is that it grounds me and brings me back to earth where I belong. It reminds me of what I live on and from. It reunites me with the matter under the metaphors. Thought is fed; revelations take place. A walk is a little life. Being sometimes weary, scratched, stung, hot, cold, wet, muddy — even scared or lost — is all part of it. That too is the work of the man in brown. His compelling reality show.

Old Whitehill, 2008

OLD WHITEHILL

In the parish of Tackley, in the county of Oxfordshire, England, the World, the Universe, an ancient hamlet lies to the south of the main village. It would be wrong to say 'the parent village', since the hamlet is the older place. It's known as Whitehill or White Hill, the variation persisting despite the attempts of officialdom — 'Is that one word or two?'— to tie it down. I live in Old Whitehill, the addition distinguishing us from Lower Whitehill, whose two attractive but nonetheless parvenu dwellings date back a mere couple of centuries.

Old Whitehill — Wihthille, Wythull', Yihthille, Visteull', Wistull, Wichthulla, Wi(h)cthill, Wicthull(e), Wichthilla, Wyhtulle, Wycthille, Withulla — is at least a thousand years old. (As with species, so with names, we were once richer, more various.) I say 'at least' advisedly, because as with my house, which appears on a map of 1608, there is no reason to suppose that the place began a named life in the very year, 1004, when Wihthille first appears on a document. Only four households now remain, but it was once a larger, south-facing settlement on a rise above the River Cherwell, and the outlines of its house-platforms are still just visible under the pasture, beside the deep cleft of the hollow way that ran beside them. Oxfordshire has a number of these deserted mediaeval village sites, or DMVs, and historians disagree as to why they declined, some putting it down to agricultural depression, others to the plague. Forty years ago when I moved here, the scant remains of one stone house still stood above ground, and I remember someone from the village telling me that her mother was born there. When even that was cleared away, for some years a misshapen pear tree remained, long past bearing fruit, a memory of a garden.

The name is said to mean 'curved hill', and its curved line against the sky means we lose the sun a little early, but the line makes up for it, and the sunsets we can watch above it. A friend who wore bow ties at twenty and knew his art and his antiques gazed appreciatively from our kitchen window once and pronounced it to be 'like a Rubens' bottom'. A part of the west side appears on the map as Pound Hill, once a fenced area or pound where strayed cattle were kept until called for. Now if cows are in the garden or sheep in the lane you just pick up the phone. No-one seems to refer any longer to Pound Hill, although until a few years ago the electricity company, seeming rather likeably and improbably to be carrying a folk memory, used to put it on our bills. It is now crowned by a small spinney of mixed trees, which I remember being planted as saplings. The man who planted them is dead now, and last week we took home from there a huge fallen branch of sycamore and cut it up for the stove.

The grassy slopes are a great place for sledging. On our single day of snow this winter I heard Blakean shouts of glee on the cold air, and there were the children, bright-scarved and hatted, struggling up and swooping down as my own used to do, and despite a touch of sadness for my own youth and my grown and gone children, I had a sense that still it was possible for the right thing to happen in the right time and place, despite so much being *not* right with the world.

In summer it's a good place to lie a while in the dark propped to watch the fiery streaks of shooting stars in the Perseids. In August 1999 we sat there to watch the eclipse of the sun. The light became weirdly greenish, and it grew palpably colder. Swallows and martins twittered anxiously and flew more slowly, uncertain what was going down. One flew close by us as though it couldn't see, and as the light dimmed to a grey-dark gloom it did feel as though one's eyes were failing. The idea that Light was failing seemed harder for the brain to believe.

From the cottage I can set out like Bunyan's Pilgrim, with my 'face from my own door', in all four directions; though if you go south, into the deserted village, then technically you are trespassing. When we first moved in we were given permission by the then farm manager to walk there, provided we told strangers to be off, and I have quietly availed myself of the former, over the years, and ignored the latter — apart from in the unhappy time of foot and mouth, which luckily we escaped. Various stiles and gates have come and gone: at present you need to climb over a gate, and you find yourself in the deserted village, looking down at a line of willows and the rushy River Cherwell. When the sheep are in here it's straight out of the twenty-third psalm. Northwards a path runs through a field which for some years has been set-aside, but which at times has been a wheatfield, with its thin line of path like in a Samuel Palmer painting, and at times cattle pasture, startling me on the first occasion before I realised what the thumping and harrumphing was, so close to the house. It goes to a footbridge over a stream and into Peter's Spout Ground, and thence across a field known at the Painthouse, or Penthouse, to Tackley (Tachelie, Taccheleia, Tacchele, Takkelea, Takele, Takeley(e), Tackele, Takkeley, Thakele, Thackelay, Tacle, Takley, Tackle, Takla, Tuckley). West takes me up the hill on a minor road, a little sunk between banks, one that is crossed by badger trails, and which, as often as it is resurfaced soon again gets a line of restorative grass growing up the middle. A few days ago, without notice, a guy in a van came and put up a sign saying that it was a 'Restricted Byway' and illegal to drive down except for access. I think he must have been from the Amblers' Association. And lastly to the east, the way I most often take, the lane becomes a track, passes under the railway bridge and on to what is known as 'The Arches', a place of local resort in summer, at quiet times a good place to loaf and watch for a kingfisher. On New Year's Eve one year I caught my breath at the sight of a water rail paddling quietly across from one bit of cover to another. They are not too uncommon, just wary. I had lived here for thirty years before seeing one. One Christmas day we surprised a green sandpiper there. I favour its folk name of martin-snipe, which perfectly captures the way it combines house martin and snipe as it flies.

On occasion, including in the late summer of 2004, I've had a spell of waking early and walking before breakfast. It's a time for being solitary, for slipping out of the house to find something that by eight o'clock will have vanished into dailiness. Almost invariably if you do meet anyone else they too are alone. A fisherman, a dog walker, the occasional jogger. At half past five on the first morning the sky is blue with white sweepings. It is chill and misty, and the earth is dark and wet from last night's rain. In the pasture by the river all but one of the black-and-white cows are sitting down. There are a few mottled grey-pink clouds in the west, but I am heading east, towards the Arches, towards the apricot light.

A rabbit bounds across the lane and into the wheat. A line of gossamer — eight feet long at least — is strung across the lane on a slant, between the hedge trees and the crop, catching the light. When I come close to it, it is shadowed and I can no longer see it, so I have to guess where it is to straddle it successfully. I don't want to break anything, including the stillness, the intactness of things. Five ducks fly over, not high, but purposeful and straight. The wheatfield is an encampment, completely filled with small, classic webs. Trees drip. It's too bright now to see well ahead. The track is wired all the way down. I've stepped over at least half a dozen lines, and there are verticals too, hanging down from a height. Lofty, my friend's black fell pony, and another horse, a white one, are awake and standing. The sun's rays are shafting through the poplars onto the river. The five small goats eye me autistically. Below the bridge are poised large brown fish, tails forked like a red kite's. Ducks quack very quietly, out of sight in the reeds. Drips from the willow make small rings on the surface. Plumes of mist rise in the early light, and two swans go stately by. The mist is the colour of marigolds. Our minds package colours so dully, compared to the rich facts — it takes a Picasso to show us that flesh can appear green. Children see it. My grandson, waking in the night once in a city, and seeing snow falling in streetlight, said 'I never saw snow before: I did not know it was orange!' On the way back I notice a new plaque on the railway bridge. It states with unintentional irony that this is 'Little Whitehall' and tells how far we are in miles and chains from the buffers at Paddington. It reminds me of the milestone in Richard Jefferies' essay *Meadow Thoughts* that told him how far he was from London in a deep countryside where such information seemed even more irrelevant.

Next morning the sky is other. The sun is silver-gilt, filtering through high cirrus cloud, fashioned into little repeating curves such as waves make on sand. A pheasant calls, and then a deer barks, a last strayed reveller of the night. Today I start out northwards across the set-aside. A young wren perches and then re-perches on the stems of the ragwort and willow-herb, keeping just a few yards ahead of me. I can smell urine and meadowsweet. A buzzard is calling but I can't see it yet. The west becomes increasingly blue. A yaffle calls. I cross the footbridge at the corner of Peter's Spout, and onto the line of Akeman Street, the Roman road, and then duck through the gap in the minimal fence of short chestnut palings to have a look at the lake.

Very occasionally the gap is mended, in a rudimentary fashion, with loose branches. But it will be re-opened almost at once, and you get the feeling of an unspoken accommodation. The small lake is the end of a chain of eighteenth-century fishponds, now relatively neglected, belonging to the Big 'Ouse, and if you step quietly up the bank behind the big chestnuts, where one year nuthatches nested, you can often see a soothing tableau of species such as you get in a Ladybird book. A grassy path runs round and on out of sight further into the park, and set back from that are old, tall trees. The pond itself is reedy at the edges, but not stagnant, the water is always flowing through. Dabchicks like this secluded place, though they dive at the least human sound, and once or twice in winter I have seen a pair of gadwall here. Today there are two adult and two juvenile coots, three or four mallard and a moorhen. A dog! It hasn't seen me yet and it isn't barking, but my guilty instinct tells me I'm outta here, even if I am only poaching intangibles to feed my soul. The dog was too, I guess. He must have come in here off his own bat, because I can now see what must be his owner, outside the fence, heading back blamelessly towards the village. On a fallen branch there's a yellow powdery fungus or mould of some kind, so bright that I thought at first it was powder paint.

I turn back and when I reach the Arches the two swans are there. Today they have seven large grey cygnets with them, all paddling, dipping and preening. Along the bank, at intervals, are tall clumps of yellow flowers of the daisy family — some kind of hawkweed? — interspersed most beautifully with contrasting blue clumps of forget-me-nots. The oak by the gate into the Long Meadow always looks empty, but on close inspection there's often something there. Today it proves to be full of tits and chaffinches. There's still mist at the far end of the meadow but slowly it melts away, and on my return the sun is quite warm on my back. A lark 'hangs singing, singing, singing, over the wheatfields wide', just as in one of the poems I so loved as a child in outer London, before I had ever heard a skylark, and which helped form my determination to live in the country as soon as the choice was my own. We sometimes went to the country on Sundays, and I knew what Rossetti meant when she said that one day in the country was worth a month in town. But it wasn't enough.

A bright green fern grows from the ugly concrete railway bridge, and in the same way, on the sewage works, an unlovely place made lovely by birds, there are pied and grey wagtails, a yellowhammer, and a young robin still lacking its red breast. And there are some starlings, which for some reason hardly ever come in the garden now, let alone nest under the tiles, as they used to. One young one, perched above the rest on the spokes of a wheel, seems to burn like a phoenix in the morning sun.

The sky next morning is evenly overcast. A rabbit scampers along the field edge of the track, and I can see the ears of another in the sewage works compound. Today there are no bullocks in sight to get excited by my arrival, so I get over the fishermen's stile and into the narrow field by the river that they call Hog's Bottom. Strictly speaking there is no footpath there, but fisherman use it, and as for the rest of us, I don't think anyone minds. A moorhen is startled at finding me so close, and takes off with a long trail of weed hanging from its beak. Halfway along there is the remains of a fire and a scatter of plastic bottles, cartons, bogrolls, wrappings of various kinds. And the soft yellow rotting wood has been hacked out of one of the old willows that line the bank. Anger rises in me and bitter reflections, but when I next walk by, having quite forgotten to bring the plastic sack into which I was going to clear it all up, I find that someone else has already done it.

At the Arches insects hover an inch or two above the water, paired with their dark reflections. A bird of prey that I can't identify is flying towards me up the Long Meadow carrying something in its claws, and then it veers away. I walk back by way of Mill Lane, enjoying the greeny-white flowers, green and red berries, and small prettily indented leaves of white bryony spread over the thick hedge that yellowhammers like. A red-brown small bee sits on a mauve scabious flower, and there are still a few blossoms of white campion among the many seedheads. A far-off dot in the sky swims closer and reveals itself as a swift. A bird landing on the bareish top of a tall hedge tree proves to have a brick-red gorget — a linnet! Once common round here, this is the first I've seen in perhaps ten years. The traveller's joy has attracted a crowd of hoverflies. Rose hips are still green. Above the garden and the set-aside there's a bubbling and twittering of swallows. A thrush skulks in the hedge, secretive, so unlike the thrushes of the Scilly Isles, that will hop almost into the houses, that it's hard to believe it's the same species. Blackbirds too are much warier here than in the suburban parks and gardens of my childhood.

The following morning the sky is grey and even more dense. The air feels cool and clammy. Hirundines are on the wing, the cattle up and feeding. Pearly petals of bramble lie on the track. No leaf stirs. A flock of about twenty long-tailed tits and plenty of other tits and finches are active between the railway bridge and the sewage works. It's a sunless stretch, always puddled, defying different people's repeated attempts over the years to drain or surface it. Swallows take mud from there for their nests, and the elegant yellow-bellied grey wagtails find something to eat. In March the dank and scrubby banks, often made drearier by an abandoned wrapper or beer can, are beautiful with white, pink, mauve and dark purple violets, all sweetly scented. There is always plenty of insect life in the elms, which is what attracts the birds. One year a couple of chiffchaffs hung around there the whole winter, and it's often a good place to see a goldcrest. The trees are wound round with ivy, and it's that that's keeping them up. They're dead on their feet, and being shallowly rooted a big wind always brings one or two down, when they are soon sawn into three or four lengths by us and barrowed home to go into the stove. There's some regeneration, but they never reach a great height before they sicken again. Those of us who can remember what the countryside looked like with live elms won't last forever either. And in the last month, just before this book goes to press, the elms have been cut down, and the particular atmosphere of that dank lane changed forever. At the same time, Peter's Spout Ground has been planted with a double line of poplars.

There are no webs today, it's as though they had never been. On a wild rose, a robin's pincushion. The old station house has recently been demolished — there are no staff now — but the overgrown garden remains, and there's still a loud familiar chirping of house sparrows from the hedge, not yet used to the fact that their house has gone. In one of the gardens what earlier looked like an over-elaborate protective contraption over a marrow plant is now justified by the largest slug I've ever seen sitting on top. A single web, the sort like a small hammock, is slung in the angle of an umbel-stalk. It grows murkier by the moment. Small whitey-brown moths flit in the vegetation. There are white nuts on the hazel. A neighbour from the village, out walking with her dog, has seen lots of tiny frogs crossing the footpath.

I enter the thorny tree tunnel at the corner of Peter's Spout, and the warm scent of meadowsweet — and the sound of water. I stand listening, and don't at once realise it is a heavy shower. It is so sudden, and the overarching trees protect me from it so completely. It droops the tall weeds over the narrow path and leaves them drenched. I walk back sopping-trousered between purple vetch and yellow vetch and willowherb and thistles.

Next day the sky is blue once more, and the air fresh. Insects are catching the light above the track and the sun glints off the wet grass. A rabbit crosses, moving just as Beatrix Potter described, going 'lippity—lippity—not very fast'. Two green woodpeckers are anting on the bridge. For a moment I don't see Sue's Lofty, dark in the dark shadow under the trees. A chiffchaff was for some reason chasing a young great tit through the laneside elms. Maybe it too was a juvenile: sometimes I have the distinct impression that young birds arse around like human teenagers, idly stirring things up a bit, before the responsibilities kick in. But then again, for the adults, it's the moult, always a grumpy time. I blame the Dog Star. A crow's feather flutters down, as it heads reluctantly off. And they have cut the set-aside field, another mark of summer's end. Yesterday it was a teeming, adorned patch of earth, all purples and yellows and cream; today it's bleak and shorn as a convict.

And so it remains throughout autumn and winter, as you cross to the big ash tree and down the bank past the pussy willow into Peter's Spout Ground. Keats urged us to stare into water, to 'Linger awhile upon some bending planks … And watch intently Nature's gentle doings', and it's good advice; it rinses the mind. At the moment there's a stout bridge of wood and metal in place which has lasted for some years. Earlier bridges, more poetic but less robust, suffered at the hands of the current Darren, a generic name suggested by the fact that it is carved by the bus shelter. Here by the bridge at the confluence of two small streams is placed a tiny bench. It has no back; it's the simplest structure of a horizontal plank placed upon two uprights. It seats one person comfortably, two only at a squeeze, and so seems designed for meditation. Beside it a long-ago coppiced hazel has grown into a shapely tree, its slender branches almost always hung with old or new catkins. When the water is flowing fast it casts ceaseless lively reflections on the uprights of the bridge. There are stones in the bank that may have been part of the Roman ford, and in April there are clumps of gleaming kingcups.

Today the tall brown dead stalks of the marshy ground are astir in the breeze. It is late January and bright sunshine, with a sky of forget-me-not blue, but with a cold northerly air stream. The bronzing and fall of the leaves was so delayed last autumn that many still lie on the mud in their rich colour, and have yet to be trodden into dark mulch. The great beeches and chestnuts inside the park palings have the sun on their lichened upper branches, which shine greenish-gold, The sounds are the *jack, jack* of the daws in them, and, closer at hand, of blue tits and great tits in the scrub. A blackbird gives its alarm with its customary melodrama, for no reason that I can detect; and nothing seems to take much notice. The sun is doing little to thaw the ground but it beautifully glitters the rime on the flattened rushes, on the splintery crystals that have formed. As I pass along the line of Akeman Street my boots crunch through the thin ice with a positively Roman intrusiveness.

A tree fallen in the recent gale has caught on the fence and leans across the path at an angle. Just beyond is that many-years-old hole, probably originally made by Darren when the fence was new, and now used by all of us who want to sneak a glimpse of the secluded, tree-fringed lake. Another fallen tree, with vigorous thick vertical ivy stems growing upwards from it to a height of five or six feet, forms a convenient screen from which to spy on the water. This time there are four mallard drakes with their green heads dramatically ashine, but they've become aware of me and take off protestingly. A dabchick pauses a second longer and then dives, and the pond is empty. I climb back down wishing I had more fieldcraft.

The line of the path has moved a little over the years, as paths often do. A fence once crossed it here, and the walker was admitted by means of a kissing-gate, whose pretty wooden curves stand idle now and half-hidden in blackthorn and bramble, starting to rot. Now you simply pass along a narrow damp track through scrub that grows over at head-height, causing all but children to duck, and then you are out into the ancient pasture known as the Dairy Ground. It's one of the many places in this part of Oxfordshire where you can see the ridge-and-furrow patterns, caused by mediaeval ploughing, which tell you it has been pasture ever since. Water, snow and sunlight all pick the furrows out more strongly, but they are visible in any light. Today the great field has sheep in. The grass has scarcely stopped growing, but they have a circular feeder filled with hay as well. On the far side, where the field is water-logged, a hundred or so black-headed gulls are congregated, contemplating their snowy images in the sky-blue water.

Here the path divides. You can continue between wire fences along the line of the Roman Road, beside a belt of tall trees, or you can head out diagonally across the grass towards the bend in the lane by the letterbox. This latter is less used, and its line is notional rather than actual. Something makes me take it today, and I am rewarded by the sight of three lapwings — in past years there used to be hundreds — standing among the gulls. For many years too this was a famous mushroom field where on any September morning you could see people with their baskets bent over in the half-light. You had to be early to get some. The stile onto the lane is not the thick oak that will last many lifetimes; but neither is it thin planking, carelessly thrown up, too high, which will split within the year leaving exposed nails and an awkward climb. It has a serviceable step which even has some cross-hatching to prevent the foot from slipping. As I saunter down the hill and back home, a robin is singing from our overgrown hedge.

WOMEN AND IMMIGRANTS

I woke feeling free of a virus that had been penning me indoors, and so joyfully cut a sandwich and lit out. As a convalescent, ambling was not only allowed, it was positively indicated. The lane underfoot is puddled from all the rain there's been, and in the puddles float the little corpses of yesterday's dancing mayflies. It's cloudy and overcast still, with the odd drop, and there's a small warmish breeze in which the cow parsley waves a little desolately. It could go either way. The may blossom is over the top. The breeze carries a medley of birdsongs and calls. I can pick out great tit, and chaffinch. I must be the slowest learner ever, but my pleasure in adding a few new ones each year is all the greater because it doesn't come easily. There's a yellowhammer's song — and there's the bird, on the bare twigs at the top of an elder. Here's a lark ascending, and here comes my first swift of the day. The presence of larks, after they had all-but vanished, puts heart into me, but they are saying that, although better farming practices are helping them now, they and song thrushes will move north as the heat increases and their food supplies dry up. The field to my left is planted with beans, and in bean years I always recall the poet John Clare's love of the spotted flowers with their sweet, clean scent, a restorative smell. And the beans themselves seem benign, recalling the nitrogen rhyme I learned at school:

Peas and beans and clover, lupins, lucerne and tares
Are all worth attention for the virtue that is theirs …

I wonder what happened to tares. The track is horseshoe-printed all the way to the Arches. I hope it's a fortunate sign. A cuckoo calls, at a distance and once only. Its call is the salt now in the Maytime dish: at one time it seemed almost the staple.

My friend Sue overtakes me on her bike, coming to see to Lofty, her fell pony. We haven't met up for a while, and she gets off and walks with me as we cross the river and then we continue to stand at the entrance to Lofty's field in sisterly talk, grateful to the spirit as this May rain was to the earth after a strange, dry April. A pair of goldfinches fly into the hedge, and Sue says she saw them yesterday too, and perhaps they are nesting. After we part I go on across the canal and up Mill Lane, past Jane's canalside tearoom — chairs on the grass — and her 'shop' and fertile cornucopic garden and smallholding. Chickens run about free, and sometimes there are spotted pigs, and a sweet-faced Jersey cow with a mellow bell. You can indeed shop, from a pretty painted boat: there is bacon, cheese, cake, jam, veg … But it is more like stepping into her dream. It's as though she had a magic wand to make it all appear: she rarely acts busy.

The earliest hedge roses are out on the sunny side of the track, and the sun itself shines out briefly and some blue sky appears. Swifts shriek and twist more wired than ravers, but in complete control. From the steep wooded bank above the old limestone quarry sound chiffchaff, gruff jay and peaceful woodpigeon. People from Tackley used to walk to work in the quarry, sometimes on a little wooden causeway across the field to the river, which was always getting washed away. When it was too flooded they had to walk the five miles, all the way round by road, and back again at the end of the day. After the quarry went out of use nature began to reclaim it. Barbed wire and warning notices appeared, and it became an exciting if rather dangerous place where fossil hunters ventured, and boys on bikes drawn by the forbiddenness. Now it has been made into a local nature reserve, and from a seat at the top you can look out over a wide vista of the Cherwell Valley. I sit for a while, a cloud of insects above me, but so far I don't seem ready for them to eat. One of the perks of being an ambler is that you sweat less than your fast walker. A buzzard sails into view, and a train slides through the valley with a deep, echoing hoot. Due west my house is hidden in trees, but I can see my neighbours' which is at the top of the opposite rise. Far down on the quarry floor, too far to tell if it's nature study or exercise, two women are teaching a primary school class. Whichever it is I feel glad that these children have this place as part of their day, as part of their life in this locality. There's a cork lying in the grass, near the seat. O.K., they should have taken it home; but it shows that people enjoy this place, and use it, and celebrate in it. The rare dragon's teeth, with their lovely subtle pale yellow peaflowers, are already in bloom. The species is called *maritimus*, but we couldn't be further from the sea. No-one is sure how they came here: maybe in a heap of spoil. The wild strawberries too are in flower, with the promise of their tiny sweet fruits. The bee orchids are not due out for another few weeks. There's a big patch of blue bird's-eye, and then almost at once I see a small blue butterfly, as though one of the flowers has taken off.

As you come into Kirtlington, a solar panel has recently appeared on one of the roofs. But there is also a posted planning application for five new houses. And there you have it: some of us are trying to be 'green', but all of us have to live somewhere, and we are too many, as the poet George Oppen (among others) identified way back in 1968 in his book *On Being Numerous*. And we are too richly needy. The village pond has mallards, and white water-lilies, and yellow flags. The village shop and post office is a pleasant hive, though, predictably and insanely, threatened with closure. If instead the main road were to be closed, or better still if all cars were to be disabled at a stroke, maybe of Jane's magic wand, the rural peace and beauty of this place, like many others, is just waiting to be revealed. We seem to drive about looking for something that, were it not for the cars, is here already. Or we fly, the drone of aircraft drowning out the music of the birds, invading the quiet. A few weeks ago one crashed to the ground a mile from here, an alien burning thing of horror. But instead of outlawing such monsters, or at least making them rare and special, we've carted it away and mended the blackened, flattened dry-stone wall and gone on as before. In fact they've even applied to extend the runway, to accommodate larger planes.

I drop in on my friend Jill, who must be close on ninety but still visits would-be immigrants in the notorious nearby Campsfield House. 'People say, "How kind you are",' she says ruefully, 'but you can tell they don't want them!' She moves on to a rhapsody on her Spanish daisies, one of the least spectacular flowers in her garden, but a favourite. Perhaps she thinks of them too as immigrants. And she asks what I think of these — some dainty yellow bells I can't quite place, with fringy leaves. 'Weeds!' she says, 'Corydalis.' But we agree that we like them, and that they can stay.

When I set off again, fortified by coffee and by Jill's spirit, the breeze is stronger. 'Blowing up for rain!' my mother used to say, taking the phrase from the old salts she used to love, on the East Anglian coast, before grey dementia took all her colourful speech. Perhaps that came into my mind because of the East Anglian names of parts of this horsy domain. Signposts point mysteriously to Cley and Blakeney. It's a common quirk, not confined to colonial America and Australia, for people to name their houses after some loved place elsewhere — Lamorna, Loch Lomond — and it may mean that one of a couple has given up a place to be with a person they loved more, although in that case the name is a permanent assertion of their sacrifice. It may be historical — a friend of mine moved into a house already called Llandaff, and has kept that Welsh marker in the middle of Oxfordshire rather than make another change. A bit of me always feels rejected by such namings, as though here is being compared unfavourably with there, but maybe I can learn from Jill and welcome the mix that we always were but are undoubtedly more acceleratedly becoming.

Crowcastle Lane is tarmacked as far as the Stud, and its tall, thick, old hedges are kept very kempt. Swallows are arrowing low as they do in this weather, and dandelion clocks are sodden like wet fur. A large greenish brimstone on the wing, which means it is a female. And as I pass by one of the barns someone is tinkering with a tractor and straightens up and greets me, and it is again a female, a girl pink-cheeked and healthy-looking as women always seem to do who have found their place in the still largely male preserve of outdoor work. I recall meeting again after many years a woman I had been at college with — I think she read history. I remembered her as fragile, nervous, uncertain. Now she was transformed into a strong and relaxed person, who appeared to be in rude health, and who carried an aura of content. I asked what she did now, and she said, 'I am a gardener. I am out of doors all day long. When I get in, I am too tired too read.' The latter was said more in apology in case I should find her bucolic, than in any real regret.

Beyond the Stud the hedge is more rangy, and trails of briar and bramble hang down from it. Back in the 1970s I can remember there being a yellowhammer's nest here every few yards, and there are still yellowhammers now; though like all the farmland birds, they are fewer. A crow flies at a kestrel and the kestrel sheers off, a little lazily, and hovers a bit further away. In the dip ahead there is the walled garden at Northbrook, tantalising because being unable to hover you can't see into it.

The canal and the river run side by side here, and the crossing is an ancient one, a stout and lovely stone bridge, and a slightly raised path, stony under the pasture grass, leads back into Tackley parish beyond. There is often a kingfisher's nest here, but I see none today, nor the grey wagtails that often whisk around the stones at a bend in the river. The old bridge is thickly covered with ivy, but there is a small bald patch where passers-by have been drawn automatically to lean and gaze. Ash, alder and sycamore trail to the surface of the water on one side, and on the other a willow stretches a branch almost all the way across. On the Tackley side you are still a long way from the village, and in much younger days I had my greatest walking scare here, not in the backwoods of British Columbia but a mile or two from home, when a bunch of probably lagered-up lads decided to molest me. As I recall there were six or seven at least, running round me like young bullocks, and I wouldn't have escaped if they'd persisted, but I kept going, and after a while they thought better of it. The experience put me off this walk for a while. On another occasion, some years later, I watched at a distance in horror as a group of young people leapt a bull, like mythical lithe adolescents from a Greek vase. It had the same air of a ritual. And then recently, in just the same place beside the river, a group of young people were sitting in a circle, not picnicking, but as though at some kind of meeting. I gave them a discreetly wide berth, wondering if this is the meeting place of some kind of secret society. I'm not superstitious (though of course I greet lone magpies) but I can't help wondering if there is something weird about that spot that excites young blood.

Today there are no humans, only the cream bullocks and the black. I brace myself for the encounter: but they are grazing intently, moving steadily forward, and take no notice of me at all. I go through a well-made, solid gate which has a small plaque advertising its provenance in the Eynsham Sawmill, and up the track to the Black Bridge, which crosses the railway line. And at last! The bird I've been missing and hoping for all day — a whitethroat. First heard, and hesitantly identified by its song, and then seen, singing on a rose. I listen out for the chiffchaff, in March, and the occasional willow warbler, less common round here than formerly; and a blackcap has been singing well in our unkempt garden for weeks now; but this I've still awaited. A dark pink rose, and then a dark blue-green damselfly. And the whole landscape a composition in white and yellow, over the green: may blossom and buttercups, cow parsley and mustard flowers. The track runs along the top of the field, and now the Cherwell valley is below again, and the famous oxbow loop in the river, used as an illustration in geography textbooks.

A small strip of meadow above the railway has been spotted and saved from 'improvement', largely due to the quiet, knowledgeable ministrations of two women, excellent amateur botanists, and is now designated a local nature reserve. The local branch of the W.I. put some money into setting it up. I sit on the bench (Eynsham Sawmill again) to eat my lunch, and see again what is probably the same buzzard I saw from the Kirtlington side. It makes its way north along the valley, and meanwhile a cormorant is following the river south. Occasionally a moorhen calls, and three or four mallard take off in a gun-dodging curve. Another train goes through. The interpretation board tells us that there are over a hundred wildflower species, fifteen sorts of grasses and twenty types of butterfly. I'm a very indifferent botanist, but I potter about and find some sainfoin in flower, a nice obvious pink spike, and one of their 'indicator' species that you find only in 'settled unimproved limestone grassland'. I recognise the leaves of salad burnet, which is another. The cowslips are gone over, and cow wheat is beginning to come into bloom. The pyramidal orchids, and all the other specialities, are still to come. And then I catch a sweet sound even more welcome for being nowadays less common here — the quiet, pretty downward cadence of a willow warbler, just audible from the scrub at the bottom of the slope.

At the top of the track known as Crecy Hill (locally pronounced Greasy) is a smallholding based on a caravan. I hear a cockerel as I approach. The door of the van always seems to stand open, and the gnomes and plaster birds and pigs and bright tubs of flowers all have a cheerful welcoming look. There are various kinds of livestock and sometimes cage-birds, and any number of subsidiary shacks and vans suggesting rural operations. A young old man, in a hat and a waistcoat, is often to be seen, presiding. I know his name, but I prefer to think of him as Goodfellow. I suppose he won't really be there for ever, but he has been there, and been the same age, for as long as I can remember.

I greet him and go on down and through the village, and out into the fields again, and spend a few minutes sitting on the bench by the footbridge into Peter's Spout Ground, where the vegetation is growing up and beginning to get its summer smell of mint and meadowsweet. The yellow flags are out. When I first moved to Tackley, forty years ago, I saw a notice inviting parishioners to join the parish council in walking the footpaths, which I did, and was the only woman in the party. One of the councillors, a thatcher and part-time Methodist preacher, waded into the marsh and picked half a dozen of the wild yellow irises and presented them to me. He was an old man, and an old-fashioned one: gallantry of that kind was on the wane even then. Probably we didn't quite know then that we shouldn't pick the wild flowers. Plenty of women walk the paths now, and sit on the parish council. There are new houses, but the village, in a bowl a mile off the main road (still too close when the wind comes from there and brings its traffic noise) is not too radically changed. I hope people still feel as welcomed.

The shapely, dainty hazel that grows at the confluence of two small streams or ditches, is reflected in the water. On the surface are the water skaters, visible only by their wake. Amanda comes by with her dog Taffy, hurrying to be there for school-out. I pat his head and he doesn't bark at me. Friends' dogs are different… I pick up a long thin fallen branch of beech, balancing it on my hip, and head for home and the kettle.

WALKIN' IN THE RAIN

Today I came across something that startled me. It's Whit Sunday, a time for astonishment — although pagan as I now am I didn't realise that till the afternoon. It rained all day, which was needed, but the wind blew as well, and every time I thought I'd go for a walk anyway I changed my mind as soon as I opened the door. It wasn't that as in the famous opening of *Jane Eyre*, 'There was no *possibility* of taking a walk that day'. We are, in some ways, made of sterner stuff than our Victorian great-great-grandmothers — or at any rate we've got better kit. It just wasn't very inviting. So instead I started to look through some old notebooks, and went for old walks in my head. On 8 April 1983 it seems I was on the Greek island of Poros. Unusually for me, I remember some of that holiday quite well: it was one of our more successful ones. There were wild flowers everywhere, and not yet many other holidaymakers. The sea, if you were English, was just warm enough to swim in. It still felt rural: I have just looked at today's pictures on the web and recognise nothing. We hit on the idea, two parents and two kids, of letting each in turn choose how we all spent a day, and it worked out brilliantly. My choice was arguably a bit of a cop-out — it involved him taking the kids off while I loafed about with *Flowers of Greece and the Aegean* and wrote passing thoughts in my notebook. Well, it was my day to choose; and being a hands-on, stay-at-home mum the rest of the year I felt I was entitled. I decreed that we were all to meet up for supper at the taverna among the pines at the top of the hill. The notebook doesn't explain any of this. The entry only says:

> Agreeably hot but with breeze. Sitting by path up thru trees to the interior. An orchard to one side with a fig and an apple at the edge and some kind of tree with long flat catkins. Animal bell and buzzing and chirping. Big daisies, big ants. Small candelabra of green spurge. Oranges and lemons are suns and moons. *When you study human nature you are studying adaptation to hostile psychic conditions.* What is a healthy habitat? Innocent grassy droppings of a donkey. Light thru sunroses.

The bit that startles me is the comment on humankind. I believe I must have been thinking semantically. I know a little Greek — or at least I did then — and my then husband is a Hellenist. (His chosen day took us across to the mainland to visit Epidaurus, where I wrote: 'Lizards in the sanctuary. A maze. Curative dreams. Tasselled hyacinths. Heard a cuckoo.') Anyway, when I wrote of hostile psychic conditions, psychic definitely meant 'of the soul'. And today the word 'adaptation' worries me so much that despite the rain I put on my waterproof and wellies and set out forthwith, because I suddenly re-remember that whatever the weather the outdoors is always my church, my library, my sanatorium.

Binoculars and notebook are equally out of the question, so I'm left with the unmediated encounter between the outer and the inner. A single clump of poppies at the track's edge draws my eye. I pine for a whole field of them to stoke my fire with their colour. The rain brings out certain smells: the field beans that the poet John Clare loved, a spicy balsam poplar and, where the water comes churning through the sluice, that sweetish, slightly fetid smell, compounded of who knows what, that I associate with the pleasures of boating on the Thames, but which isn't usually evident here on a rural stretch of its tributary the Cherwell. Two swans hold themselves poised and still in the current, live, strong and beautiful. White on a grey day. The rain tip-taps on my hood, and beyond that is the shivery sound of the wind in the poplars. And a blackbird is singing — there it is, at the very top of a tallish ornamental evergreen in the garden of The Pigeons. The Pigeons was once a pub, and a few years back the oldest Tackley dwellers could remember walking down Mill Lane and across the field of a Saturday evening 'to take our pleasures there'. Lemonade, as often as not.

A blackbird. We tend not to stop, especially in the rain, to listen or to draw one another's attention to it. It is the loveliest music, simple and yet rich, and we take it for granted. If our spring is not yet silent, it is a good deal emptier. In many parishes thrushes have left their pulpits vacant. Linnets have become scarce hereabouts. If blackbirds went too we would no doubt adapt, but at what unregistered cost?

We have been watching anxiously, Jeremy and I, for the visitations of a pair of house sparrows to our garden feeders. A single pair, when formerly a whole tribe of them cheeped cheerfully in and out of our eaves, bathed in the dust of the lane, enlivened the brambles. They were rather like blackberries in fact, common, cheap and cheerful, giving a subliminal message of hope and abundance. Sometimes now a day or two pass without our seeing either of these survivors. Then one or the other returns. Finally, a few days ago, three fledglings appeared, lined up on a branch agitating their wings or hunkered down on the outside window sill while the parents worked their socks off. 'Hopping casement-comers,' Thomas Hardy called them, glad as we were to see them, though he couldn't have imagined them so scarce. This time, this one sparrow had 'found her an house'.

At Pigeons Lock I stand on the canal bridge for a while, watching the rain dimpling and dimpling on the opaque water, and then turn for home. On the way back I wonder about the tree house that's appeared in the garden behind The Pigeons. It has the air of a dream realised. The wooden slats up the trunk invite, though I have never yet seen or heard children in occupation. It is as one imagined —before the film, when one still could imagine — an elf lodging in *The Lord of the Rings.* And the curious thing is that the wire fence just by it is trodden to the ground as though by the exiled, longing and breaking in to reach a home. Many householders increasingly wall the rest of the world out with high hedges and electronic devices and even warning notices. It's not confined to England: my builder and after so many years now old friend Peter has just been describing to me the multiply locked and walled housing compounds of Alicante (mainly lived in by Brits it's true). But there's been no attempt to fill this gap, and I almost believe it might have been done from the inside, perhaps not intending random passers-by actually to come in and enjoy the arborial retreat, but as a symbol of openness, of possibility. A gesture to fragrance the divisive, exclusive air that property so commonly gives off. I could go and knock at the door (the front door) and ask. They are after all almost my nearest neighbours, to the east. But I'm afraid of a rebuff, or a prosaic explanation. I would rather cherish my hope.

A bank of small pink cranesbills catches my eye freshly. Some people will only go a round walk, claiming that it bores them to cover the same ground. But it is really only the poverty of our observation that records a dull sameness. Apart from the different angle of vision, which to my eye transforms everything, there is always the possibility of a fox or a muntjac you wouldn't otherwise have seen, or a different bird event.

White campion glows very white, with that kind of luminosity that white flowers with any breadth of petal often have. Here are the first meadow cranesbills I have seen this year, in their pristine blue, before they have taken on the purplish tint of age. Ducks and wagtails are at home in the rain, and there are plenty of corvines plying raggedly about in the wind, even if the smaller birds are more hidden. The young still need to be fed though, and look even more draggled than usual in their provisional plumage, as they wait for the hard-worked parents to keep it coming.

Back indoors, with a cup of tea and the stove lit, I return to the old notebooks. And back on Poros another entry perhaps throws some light on my sudden philosophical turn. I have recorded (in the Greek whose resonances I was so much enjoying) a public information notice close to Aliki beach. Translated it means something like:

> I am a place of health and beauty and peace.
> Protect me against catastrophe.

The words in Greek are longer and seem to have deeper meaning. They seem as though they ought to be spoken by the chorus of a Greek tragedy. They have that ominous ring.

Not far from here are the ancient hay meadows at Yarnton, managed by the local Wildlife Trust. A large part is called Pixey Mead, which I take to be Pucksy, or in other words a favourite haunt of the Man in Brown. Invariably when you step through the hedge you run the gauntlet of human excrement, pages of pornography, latex gloves, syringes. Or at best merely fast food wrappings and drink cans. The meadows have never come under the plough, and the beauty of them is understated, rich, intense. In early June the tallest plant is a deep purple-red that appears black at a distance, the round flower-heads of the great burnet. Devil's-bit scabious (one of the puck-named, Robin Goodfellow plants, like ragged robin and herb robert) shows a dark lilac at the next level. There are innumerable plants, and many species, feathery grasses, grasses that quake like miniature aspens, yellow composites that are definitely not dandelions, drifts of meadowsweet. I know only a few by name. Small moths flit pale, beetles gleam. And over all like the barbarians at the gates the sound of the A40 traffic is so loud you can scarcely hear your companion's discoveries or provisional identifications or little rhapsodies. You can scarcely hear your own thoughts. It seems, this continuous noise, to be an outrage, a violation of the meadow itself. It quite mars the pleasure, and prevents this from being paradise in the way that the machair of a Scottish island can seem to be. And yet it is so precious. In proportion to the rest of the built over and chemically devastated land hereabouts it is less than the single tress in a locket of a loved one who has died. But unlike the tress it is alive.

Mixed with the deep sadness at the loss of an earth that could be like this is anger on behalf of the meadow itself. How can we so carelessly destroy its peace? But then we came here by car ourselves. If the meadow at our door were like this there would be no need. The path through this meadow is scarcely trodden. Most people don't know what's here. If the Man in Brown were suddenly and puckishly to disable every car, if we were spell-stopped as in *A Midsummer Night's Dream*, what an extraordinary and lovely peace would fall, like dew for the dry psyche. We could walk in the meadow seeing and scenting like children. And as children once did we could pick a bunch and it would do no harm, there would be so many everywhere.

Sunt lacrimae rerum: there are tears for *things*. Not for transience, not for mortality: for things. Both my children walk wherever they find themselves — Phoebe currently in Moscow, and Nat in the hills and along the estuaries of North Wales. It's a way — *the* way you could say — of getting to know a patch of earth and learning to love its passing or more lasting things. It is the corollary of learning the language. The Welsh poet Bobi Jones says that paths also are a language. There is joy in things also.

Some time later I did knock at the tree-house people's door. And received a kind welcome, and climbed up into it, and an open invitation to bring the grandchildren when they were next over from Russia.

BUS ROOT

Some years ago I found an old London bus ticket inside a second-hand book. I'd forgotten how it used to be. Now, gazing at it and taking it into my hand, I remembered the rows of different coloured tickets, about one inch by two, made of an agreeably soft thick paper that was not quite card, that the bus conductors carried wired onto a board. My pleasure in them had been second only to that of going through my mother's box of wooden cotton reels, with their agreeable, reassuring taxonomy: brick red, bottle green, dove grey. And didn't something ring or click when a ticket was issued, or was that just the conductor ringing merrily to re-start the bus? There was too a kind of crude English origami, popular among little girls, by which your ticket and any others you could commandeer could be made into miniature chairs, tables and sofas…

Probably that pink ticket would now be a collector's item, to be sold separately. Certainly second-hand books — 'used' as people now call them, suggesting seediness rather than history — now often come well-dusted and even encased in plastic, efficiently frisked and relieved of letters, cuttings, leaflets, leaves, flowers and all other official and unofficial book-marks, unless these are flagged up and allowed for in the price. So the possibility of such a find is in itself a subject for nostalgia. Somewhere in me though, below the memory-line, those tickets have contributed to — almost they represent — my positive feeling for buses, which outweighed the cigarette smoke, the jolting difficulties of the stairs, the sometimes having to stand, the odd cross conductor, and fellow-passengers occasionally intimidating or unsavoury in a variety of ways. I am rooting for buses.

My parents had no car. As a child in the 1940s and '50s car journeys were for me a rare (and nauseous) event. In cars I felt trapped, hijacked. Buses on the other hand — and to a lesser extent trains — were necessary, valued, depended on. To buses, I suddenly realise, I owe a sense, which I have never lost, of being a member of the public. This was public transport, and we were passengers, not customers. My parents liked walking, and public transport connected us to public footpaths. At weekends Green Line buses took us out from suburbia into the countryside and gave us the freedom of fieldpaths and green lanes.

What sticks in my mind is the plunder — field mushrooms from Cheam, chestnuts from Richmond Park, tiny wild strawberries from Pretty Corner. Somewhere there was a hazel copse, and blackberries were everywhere. One day my usually cautious parents went on an organised Fungus Foray and discovered their wild side. After that we found and cooked parasol mushrooms, blueleg blewits, shaggy inkcaps (rather slimy, these), penny buns and once, relishing the scary unlikeliness of it, we feasted on saffron milk caps, which are orange, concave, and covered in green blotches. Although they were hard up, my parents showed no interest in growing vegetables, so I think this gathering was not so much about eking out their income as communion with nature. For the most part their life was narrow, pavement-bound, drab, unadventurous, but they had hankerings. The earth called to them, saying *Take, eat.* Mushrooms and nuts were the outward sign, but hundreds of walks that I have forgotten live in me, nourishing gratitude, love of the open air and open spaces, of weather, seasons, plants, creatures, water, earth and sky.

There were more buses to come. Honeymooning in Greece for a month or two in the sixties (the ambling boyfriend now become a husband) we would travel by bus as far as it went and continue on foot. Rattling and bouncing along to the plinking catchy corny music, rosaries a-jump on the windscreen, those beaten-in contraptions penetrated a countryside then less explored by foreigners. Crones in black, their faces furrowed fields, men with mattocks, families, livestock, us young and innocent as Start-rite kids, we were all on the sunny but stony road of life, dust our common element. We two had our backpacks, but otherwise luggage was biblical, done up in baskets and cloths. The people were poor and correspondingly generous. Oranges, melons, ouzo, were pressed on us. With even television not yet everywhere, you didn't have to be from another planet to be an alien. We knew a little Greek, and their curiosity was vast and unenglish. Where do you come from? What is it like there? Do you have the sun there? And the moon? And the Virgin Mary? Ah, (with relief, or with disappointment?) then it's the same. *You will go to the good*, the older people would call in blessing, when at the final shuddering stop we hefted our packs and set off along donkey paths into the heat and the unknown.

We were only twenty then, and further along the life-path the husband and I forked separate ways, and it's with another companion that I've enjoyed bus-ing and walking in the second part of life, on Guernsey, Texel, Tiree and the Outer Hebrides, and the interlinked, frequent, and utterly dependable network of buses criss-crossing Berlin where my daughter and her family lived for a time. (The varied and adventurous walks she was able to plan, relying on that remarkable system, for people who need to be certain to be back for school-out, would make a book in itself. Now that she lives in Moscow she is once more on the walking and public transport kick, and has her own column *Phoebe's Weekend Walks* in the *Moscow News*.)

So buses for me have been connected with feelings of holiday and romance and exploration, as well as with community and getting in touch with the life of a place more intimately than one can in a car. And now that I am a crone myself, though wearing neither purple as the poet suggested nor black like the old women of the Peloponnese, I have been presented with the freedom of my locality: a bus pass. It comes as a photo-card; and I have finally, after ten years at a stretch of gloomy passport photos, and even longer as a malevolent-looking user of the Bodleian Library, learned the importance of a smiling picture, which contributes a mite to my euphoria. Unlike me, the card is encased in hideous lavender plastic; but if it were the true, regal aubergine which (so they tell me) symbolises the celebration and acceptance of cronehood, or the deep spiritual violet associated (so I am given to understand) with the opening of one's final chakra and emergence into wisdom, I could not be more delighted. Mauve is magic. It's sometimes said that you value things more if you have to pay for them, but for me, brought up with the glamour of wild food and a relish for bargains, it's the opposite. Every time I get on board gratis I feel grateful, humbled, transported.

And free. *News from Nowhere* was first published in 1891 and was set in Oxfordshire in the early twenty-first century. For me, as it happens, that is here, and now. The hero's dream, or vision, of the future begins with a river trip for which he offers to pay; whereupon the ferryman 'laughed loud and merrily, as if the idea of being paid for his work was a very funny joke'. There are pockets of resistance, but as a society we are racing in quite the opposite direction from Morris's green socialist utopia, and unless climatic or some other disaster stops us it's hard to imagine we will turn ourselves around. So showing my bus pass is as close as I come to Morris's imagined world, and every time I do it I think of his warmth and innocence and energy and love of beauty, and of my friends Robin and Heather Tanner, artists, botanists and educators, who carried his vision in their work and lives, and am heartened.

By the time this book goes to press, us olds will be able to go free on any local bus, but for now there's a lot of small print, a bureaucratic undertone to my whiff of utopia. And even then at ten to nine you will still have to pay, even when there's plenty of room. Unless it's a Saturday or a Sunday. But here in Tackley there are no buses on a Sunday. For now you have to start or finish your journey within the West Oxfordshire District, and since Tackley is more or less enclosed by the Cherwell District, you are more or less limited to the route of the 59 bus, which is between Oxford and Banbury. My partner calls this my Route 66, after the Beat trail across America. Fortunately on Route 59 life is rich and concentrated. A few drops are enough. I don't need to go far or fast, don't need the drugs or burning up the gas, not at my age anyway. Though perhaps that world is closer at hand than I realise, because even in Steeple Aston, the next village north, old walls of dove grey stone, gardens of marigolds and sunflowers and beans, a half-term group of frisky kids are shrieking and horse-playing outside the shop, and in bold black felt-tip on the newly-painted bus shelter someone wants to let the world know that 'Damien Smith (I have changed the name) is a crack rat'.

But I should start from the Tackley shelter. It is late July.

'Deddington, please.'

'It gets there eventually, but it does it.'

The implied apology is because this bus, like two or three others each day, takes a longer route, by way of Duns Tew and the Bartons. I'm not in a hurry; I'm savouring everything in the way that you can when you're not the driver, not going fast, and are sitting high to the road. The drivers sometimes talk as they edge past each other going opposite ways down a narrow village street. 'We just seen the ol' man, you know wi' the ol' cam'ra by the garridge? You'll see 'im there…' I didn't notice him, and imagine a crazy. Though probably it's someone like me, a fellow spirit. Perhaps soon it'll be, 'We picked up that ol' gel with 'er rucksack again, writin' in 'er lil notebook…'

One meaning of the verb 'to root' is to lounge or idle about, as Walt Whitman did when he wrote 'I loafe, and invite my soul.' Or as Richard Jefferies was accused of doing by those who felt busier. Through the open window comes the tang of woodsmoke, and we pass a fairly major bonfire of tree trunks. I wonder why they aren't fuelling somebody's stove. It's a smell I associate with autumn, with my time of life. *Live,* it says, *live now.* Harvest is early this long hot summer and there's combine dust in the air. On the verges, the small pink and the great white bindweeds. White butterflies look like the convolvulus on the wing. A small procession of open-top vintage cars is going in the other direction, their hatted and scarved occupants serious and intent as though at a ritual, as perhaps it is.

The bus offers a transitional state between indoors and out. In Deddington I get out and encounter life more directly. The houses here are not the cream-grey Cotswold limestone, but a fierce golden eagle yellow, the famous ironstone of the local quarry at Hornton. From close up you can see and feel its texture. In 1933 M.V. Turner was a runner-up, with her *Story of Deddington,* in a W.I. competition, and in her dry account her praise for 'the ferruginous marlstone with visible white shells in it' stands out as loving and lyrical, brings ancient and oceanic thoughts. You will find the same effect in many an academic treatise where scholar-cred seems to demand dryness and the original passion that fuelled the research is caged in a sentence or two. And you get a similar effect in an

Iain Sinclair book, where the prevailing tone is tough, even cynical, but where usually, possibly a couple of hundred pages into it, you'll find a sentence, two at the most, of the purest, most vulnerable heart.

I enjoy my armchair walking with Sinclair, just as I enjoy such walks for real, *thoroughly.* This is something I've learned from the cheerful nature of my friend Val, herself a walker. Her glass as a rule is not just half full but pretty much up to the top, and I've come to realise recently how inspiriting her phrase is when she reports, 'we *thoroughly* enjoyed ourselves'. She always walks in company, and that, for her, is a big part of the pleasure. But we introverts who take our pleasures differently can still be thorough, if we let ourselves be open to the world. It begins at the feet and goes all the way up through the nerves and muscles until it reaches that crown chakra and comes fizzing out through one's hat. It's a complete spring-clean. Joy uses you as a thoroughfare and recreates. It reminds me of Thom Gunn's poem *Yoko* about a dog who joyfully investigates everything, a poem I love for the life in it.

An elderly man in shorts is lying under an old car, fixing it. He looks comfortable. He doesn't look poor. He is doing this for pleasure. Morris (William, that is) wouldn't have liked cars, but he liked to see work done for pleasure, and it raises my spirits too. I turn off the main road heading west down The Grove, which instead of trees now has very new and soulless houses with no wood or stone and nothing hand-fashioned about them, but which abruptly dwindles to a narrow line of baked and cracking earth between drying black fodder beans, and am out of it all.

Into it all. There are actually poppies, rarer now, growing at the path edges. Boots press actual earth, orange-yellow like the houses, although you get the feeling not many do. As mine do, the smell of pineapple rises from the low-growing mayweed. Among the poppies there are small light green spurges, mauve thistles with bees on them, white daisies with carrot-like leaves — one of that family of umbelliferous plants that each summer I mean to get to grips with and never do. Being 'slow of study' like Snug the Joiner has its advantages: there is so much more to look forward to. Next year, beetles — the easy ones anyway. After that, mosses ditto. Identification is satisfying, but so much will always remain mysterious, and marvelling, like roaring, can be done extempore.

Here are pungent plants of the mugwort family. Mugwort?

Wormwood? An old saw has it that 'A man may go forty mile with mugwort in his shoes'. A friend and I once tried it, on a long walk made wearisome by the oilseed rape planted on the paths, fiendish to walk through when tough and full-grown — and we fancied it actually did give us a new spring in our step. And here is a butterfly, I really ought to know this one — quite large but somehow elegant, pale peachy orange for the most part, with eyes on the light brown underwing. Back home I look it up — painted lady! Of course. All the way from North Africa, now looking for thistles like these to lay her eggs on, and bare earth as there is here on which to bask. I pass small knotweeds and nightshades. The odd drift of oilseed rape and oats from previous plantings, and the presence of orange ladybirds, is reassuring: these fields haven't been oversprayed. A breeze creaks the dry beans, a greenfinch wheezes, and a yellowhammer lets out its song that is bottled summer. Here are tiny wild pansies, hearts-ease.

The path leads through an old thick hedge by means of three rough wooden steps, coloured orange by the earth trodden into them, a shaded place to sit and eat, and contemplate the way ahead. A striped fly lights on my knee. This is a countryside of gentle undulations, hedged fields. The next field is sown with wheat, and the sound of the wind in it is changed to a soft sweeping. The unsown path has a sprinkling of the blue petals of speedwell, as though snippets of the sky overhead had fallen to earth, and here is a tall, handsome yellow-flowered plant of the daisy family, another that I may get round to sorting out one day. Meanwhile it is a sun-disciple, a yellowhammer of the plants. It recalls a line of the dead poet William Carlos Williams, heard on a creaky old pirated tape someone gave us, where the poet, himself old and creaky by then but still full of life, utters with slow, emphatic relish 'yellow, yellow, yellow, yellow'.

Here and there are larks, and even snatches of song, though it's late in the year for music. I hear a mewing, stop and scan the sky — and there it is, a lone buzzard circling and calling. A wren flies low out of the crop and into the hedge, ticking loud at my intrusion.

Between this field and the next the path is carried across what is at present a thin trickle of water shining below elders and tall leaning nettles by a wooden bridge, and on this the earth-stain is almost red. The way is now through pasture where sheep are grazing, and all at once a flock of twenty or thirty lapwings passes over, with a few starlings among them.

My heart lifts as it always does at the black and white twinkle and loose lapping grace of their flight. A few seconds and they are gone, and a certain emptiness returns, and the underlying sorrow for what we have done. It's a quiet time of day and of the year for birds, but it isn't just that. Lapwings, like many other species, are less common hereabouts. These fields would once have teemed with linnets and tree sparrows too.

The next footbridge takes me out of pasture, through a hedge with several tall ash trees, and into a recently ploughed field. At first there are traces of where other feet have grazed the soft dry clods, but I lose them, and am heading out blind, trying to hold a straight line. A large shapely oak stands in the brown sea like an old tall ship. I finally find my gap in the hedge and I'm back on terra firma, at Ilbury Bridge on the minor road to Duns Tew. Ilbury means yellow fort — but the Iron-age hill fort of iron-y earth, and even the mediaeval hamlet that succeeded it, are long gone. There is just a high, smooth field. I lean my belly against the hot brick of the bridge and watch the water, moving and bright but a long way down. Some blackberries in this warm spot are ripe already

The road goes gently uphill to Duns Tew, lined with old oaks, ashes and hawthorns, and huge swatches of soft thistle seed. Swallows skim the road ahead of me. The verge to either side of the entrance to Common Barn Farm has been mown for some distance, and little stonewalled flowerbeds created on either side of the gateway. I'm glad they can't annexe the whole length of roadside verge, but I enjoy the contrast, and even find something reassuring in the competence, and the urge to cultivate. Then a house for sale on the outskirts of the village boasts of having been 'refurbished', as though the ugly factory-made doors and windows were something to be proud of, and I wonder what beauties were lost. A constant source of stress which we learn to ignore, as we do noise and light pollution, is the way we have to brace ourselves against inhuman architecture.

Recently on a brief trip to Arundel I picked off the shelf an old book I'd once bought second-hand and never read before to read on the train. It was *Field Paths and Green Lanes in Surrey and Sussex* by Louis J. Jennings. Originally published in 1887, and this was its fifth edition, in 1907, so it must have been popular. As it turned out though, I was the first with this particular copy, and although it was freckled as belongs to an elderly being, I had the indescribable pleasure of cutting some of the pages with the sharp edge of my train ticket. Once or twice that has happened to me in the Bodleian Library, which feels even more like being the first explorer into a wilderness, when even the scholars haven't been before you. Jennings is fascinating in all kinds of ways. He refers to the people he meets as 'rustics'. Sometimes the apparent naivety of those days is breathtaking. He has decided opinions and seemingly no fear of expressing them, but his enthusiasms are as great and various as his dislikes. I enjoy the roundness of his assertions:

> There are few things in life better worth living for than the pleasure of starting out on foot in fair health, and with no particular anxiety pressing upon the mind, for a long day amid the beauties which Nature spreads before her true lovers by every hedgerow and brook and hillside in England.

Right on, Louis, know what you mean, man. Though I find it pretty good for loosening the anxiety too. He complains that locally-produced food is never to be had — it has all gone to London; interesting that that was the case even then, and it is one way in which things have just recently begun here and there to improve. On the other hand, his explanation of how to get the best walks 'by skilful use of the railroad' makes one's blood pressure rise at the memory of the Beeching axe. And I was rather envious of his forthrightness about what he considered to be ugly building: 'How can the man who built these have the coolness to look his fellow-creatures in the face again?'

Public transport leads to public footpaths and public footpaths, as often as not, to public houses. I have met no other human being since leaving Deddington, and a desire to be reunited with my own kind, to dispel the fantasy of being the only person left on earth after some silent but catastrophic event, mixes with the idea of a beer. I am after all out for enjoyment. And it's open! Some pubs, even quite large ones, are open only at meal times, and the walker is grateful to those who still consider their role to be that of an inn, offering respite and refreshment to the traveller, and a sense of inclusion. In The White Horse the holiday feeling is oddly intensified because the bar staff are chatting to one another in what I take to be Polish. Framed auction notices from a hundred years ago offered *74 Oxford Down Sheep, 24 head of well-bred cattle, 8 valuable horses and colts, agricultural implements, household furniture*...that too must have seemed like the end of an era. They wouldn't have had 'air freshener' then though. The drink was welcome, but I was glad to go out again from air freshener into fresh air.

And so to 'the house that stands for all'. This is what William Barnes, the open-hearted parson-poet from Dorset, called the village church, and yes, there is a trusting vicar and church wardens here, and it too is open, and the visitor is cheered by the yea-saying, by the welcome. We are thankful when there is no locked door forbidding our Larkinesque prowlings and peekings, while God lords it in there like a landowner in a Big 'Ouse, away from the *hoi polloi.* I enjoy the cool stone interior of St. Mary Magdelene, and the carved grotesques at the tops of the pillars. I buy a booklet *The Story of Duns Tew, Oxfordshire, through the Centuries* by J. Lindsay, liking its old-fashioned, longwinded title. In it I read that Ilbury Camp might once have had a temple to the Firegod, and that at his festival, the Vulcanalia, 'people threw animals into the fire instead of themselves'. Startling stuff. This goes well beyond Thoreau's quiet desperation. In the seventeenth century a serving wench was hanged for infanticide but survived it, and went on to have several more children. Tough law and tough people. In the late eighteenth century a preacher caused a stir with a sermon in which he 'warmly advocated the principles of the French Revolution'. Christianity arguably embraces liberty, equality and fraternity but, in the case of the Anglican Church, tepidly. Or perhaps not so much embraces as shakes hands embarrassedly on Sundays and then turns back to the class system with relief.

And now for the luxury of being driven home, of being able to do a non-circular walk. Buses to Duns Tew are more common than hen's teeth but not much, and I don't want to miss it. Bus stops are absent altogether. Probably a bit too French Revolutionary. But a friendly native who is sitting very comfortably in his porch with beer and newspapers lets me into the secret of where to wait. Every warm day that I come through this village I see him sitting at his open door, inhabiting. The Ridge House, where I catch the bus, has an extraordinarily thick thatch, and in it a very small, very deep window.

COUNTRY MATTERS

Much of West Adderbury is posh, as in fine old houses well-maintained, but not land-owning posh; and conscious of their rights and their health and why they live in the country, the local people have looked after their footpaths. The path I want is signposted between houses, and leads off as a clear, bare line through the wheat. The gardens on either side are slightly surreal: one has a marquee in it, and one has an elaborate structure of painted nesting boxes for chickens that seems to be modelled on the toy farm sets of my youth. Beside the stile is a little stall with boxes of eggs for sale and another box in which you're trusted to put your money. There's something touching about it and I want to buy, as I would from a child who had set up shop at the garden gate. I feel rather sorry that being at the start of my walk makes it impractical.

The path turns out to be well-used; it is not a mere weed-killered line. A young Asian woman appears, jogging, and after that a family of five with a dog. But there are signs too of the other life that is lived alongside ours like a kind of alternative universe. Dog turds are not the only ones: there are small 'currants' with what look like cherry stones in, and some curved tapering twists. Deer? Foxes?

The breeze is from the north and it brings a quite strong smell of coffee all the way from the factory in Banbury. Jeremy says he has smelled it at home too occasionally, which would mean it had travelled fifteen miles. You can smell the pineapple weed as you crush it underfoot, but the coffee is there too, inescapably. This terrain is marginal in another sense than the usual. It's not seedy or neglected hinterland: on the contrary, it's almost obsessively manicured and tidy. It's country trying very hard not to be town — a little unnatural. It follows a dream of the country, a storybook fiction where white ducks float tidily on clean ponds and never shed mucky feathers. A white-painted wooden mill whose sails don't turn round has come from the same set as the chicken-houses. But there is a risk in this. Sometimes in scrubbing away the dirt you lose the soul. You find it just slipped out quietly by the back door when people started shaking the mats too vigorously and spraying 'odour-eaters'. It occasionally feels like that to me in places managed by the National Trust. There is one dinky wooden signpost too many, or an over-gravelled path, a blank expanse of grass, or a prim cloned tea room fresh out of Ikea. Or Sark. Apparently there are people who fall in love with Sark and go there year after year. No cars, island peace, what more could you want? How to explain the soul's need of dirt, wildness, something left to chance, left to itself, just something *left*. One side of Tresco, in the Scilly Isles, is a bit the same, but at least it's easier to get off it again. When I got down that Sark cliff and the boat came for us I felt I'd escaped, got out of gaol free.

In the midst of the wheaten sea are single, beautiful trees, and by the path grow pale mauve thistles and yellow hawkweeds. And heart's-ease. The name alone is therapeutic, but the tiny perfect pansies — pensées — with their easy to overlook beauty and delicacy speak about something we need and don't realise. And they have humility: they live close to the earth.

As I plod up the gentle rise a bird flies up from the wheat. It is pale brown above and a soft primrose yellow beneath. It lands and then takes off again, and as it flies it utters a single sweet 'tseep' which I know I don't recognise, and which enables me to say later, when I've looked it up, that it is definitely a yellow wagtail, a female, as I thought. This species is one of the canaries, not literally of the ilk despite its colour, but because it warns us that something's wrong. Its numbers have dropped dramatically. It is on the conservationists' 'amber' list, and is being considered for the red. Then I hear a chiffchaff's questioning call note and a wren's irritated trill. And then there is quite a chorus of small birds' alarms which puzzle me until the striped menace of a sparrowhawk jets through. Well, if the bird/soul comparison holds, this place still has some soul after all.

Here is a small dainty white butterfly, and there a painted lady. On the verge of the minor road that crosses now some meadow cranesbill is still in bloom. Beyond that road you enter a different territory, distinctly more raffish. To the east of the now concrete path is part dingy weedy wasteland, with scrannel plants such as fumitory and bindweed, and part what looks like a bikers' circuit. Ahead are glasshouses and big old unpruned appletrees, the old order changing but not yet giving place to new. I choose the path going more to the northeast, partly to avoid the sheepdog that is barking towards me at speed, and sit among big gold wheels of straw to eat my lunch. Meanwhile the dog's owner has caught it up and they are both coming this way too. In fact the savage animal now approaches me peaceably with a stick in its mouth which I dimly understand I am to take and throw, and which I do, feeling foolish.

The path continues through rough pastures, by stile and footbridge, until it passes directly in front of a house, one of those places where you feel uncomfortably obtrusive, and up a steep and narrow and very watery slope that must be completely impassable in winter. Red and yellow bird cherries have fallen by the stile at the top. After one more field the path leads into Bodicote, but I head off westwards in the direction of Milton, wanting to have a look at the small patch of blue on the map.

Before I get to it I know it must be close by the sudden appearance of swooping house martins; and when I reach it, a small reservoir, it is a refreshing, pretty tableau for which the rough dry pastures have created a kind of thirst. A pair of swans, a moorhen or two and a coot, a small round dabchick with its even smaller chick, as well as the active martins and a greenfinch clan, with the dark green rushes and the trees in the background, all assist in fashioning a scene that recalls old paintings wherein all of nature exists side by side in harmony. The grass of the bank is pressed down as though people have sat or lain there recently, but no-one else is here now.

In the middle of the next meadow some pungently new fencing operations have left an old gate and its post standing by themselves unconnected to a fence. The gate stands open. It would make a first-rate contemporary art installation, more interesting than Tracey's famous bed to my mind, as leaving more work for the imagination. And it has the correct postmodern quality of unsettling you.

The sound of a crowd watching a game increases as I walk, and soon I turn, at the edge of an estate of modern houses, onto the Salt Way, and even more unsettling is the gate at the entrance to the estate which is freshly painted with *Your Mum Sucks Cocks.* Other people are walking along the Salt Way but in some indefinable way they are not in country mode. They are walking it as though it were a pavement. It comes out onto a trafficky road by a roundabout. I have walked to the edge of town. Bodicote Flyover Farm Shop is a kind of oxymoron. But the idea of a farm, a Little Red Hen, Farmer Giles sort of farm, is powerful. A woman comes click-clacking towards it in high-heeled sandals and thick make-up. 'Are they open?' she asks me, and is smilingly pleased that they are. She will give her family a farmhouse tea.

The bus stop's plastic timetable cover (glass is way too vulnerable these days) has been burned and melted to illegibility. To Darren everything is a scab and must be picked. I suppose if his ancestors were countrymen they might have been rick-burners. Bus times are quite small beer. But at least Captain Swing knew what he was for as well as what he was against. Recently the vandalism has increased so that I even wonder if it *is* Darren —it seems too urban. *Fuck U* has appeared in huge blue letters on the Whitehill railway bridge, and the door is wrenched off the Whitehill letter box, which must have required a crowbar at least.

Here in Bodicote a notice proposes the demolition of one of these 'ribbon' main road houses and the erection of a further thirty in the field behind. Every acre of land that is not inalienably agricultural, and some even of that, will soon have its quota. Where will the wild things go? How shall we breathe? I like the bit on the bus journey back where we are in a line of traffic stuck behind a slow, rusty tractor. As we go through West Adderbury a horse-drawn carriage is bearing a bride and groom away from the marquee'd garden.

HOLY GROUND

As you wander along the Nethercote Road in Tackley you can get glimpses of gardens down the private 'tuers' or 'twittens' between the houses; and although a writer is always a kind of gumshoe I peer today with an increased curiosity and a newly-opened eye. This is because Jeremy and I recently decided we were just about good enough bird-watchers now to volunteer for a British Trust for Ornithology survey. We've been part of the Garden Bird Watch for a long time, but this Breeding Bird Survey is a more advanced business altogether. You're allotted a kilometre square to record, and there are minutely complicated instructions about how to describe the nature of the terrain, the timing, the distances. You have to walk two 'transects', which are science's answer to ley lines — that is, they go in a straight line cross country taking no account of any natural obstacles or human routes or boundaries. Naturally for this you have to seek permission from the landowners, and with memories of my footpath activist days, and the stressfulness of bearding farmers, I approached this bit of the task anxiously. It was cheering to find that the three owners in question all gave permission readily and with interest. When it came to the surveying we probably missed or misidentified one or two things — I blame the weather, dogs, ticks, awkward fences and a vague fear of being challenged by someone who hadn't been told about us, as well as our own lack of skill. I wonder how many other bad bird-watchers do the survey, in the sense that it's used in Simon Barnes's warm-hearted, enthusiastic book *How to be a Bad Bird Watcher*. I wonder if it's a nerve-racking undertaking for others too, or whether my picture of the utterly competent, fit, expertly-garbed birder (always male, and rather like a Real Rambler — the modern form of what Louis Jennings calls 'the true pedestrian') — is closer to the mark. We're not there yet, but we're learning all the time; and we did see both tree sparrows and corn buntings, both of which are scarcer than they once were, and neither of which we'd seen for a while.

But the real revelation for me was that although our square is in easy walking distance of where we live, the landscape viewed from unaccustomed angles, from off roads and footpaths, made it almost a strange place. Private land, whether many acres or a small garden, by exclusion also limits one's vision and one's understanding of a place. When you wish to make peace, you need to try to understand the other's point of view, and here we had experienced the force of the literal meaning underlying that metaphor. It's something that stays with me. Not only do I constantly wonder what I'm missing, but I experience a distinct increase in my feelings of neighbourliness when I do know how it looks from the inside.

The Nethercote bus stop has a shelter tucked into the hedge, not an ugly transparent box with narrow plastic misericords, but one built of stone and Stonesfield slate like the older village houses, and with a proper wooden seat. The problem with it for bus travellers is that you can't see the bus coming and be ready to stick your arm out, so the only people who can relax in it are the kids, who colonised it as a hang-out from the start. Here it was that Darren came even before the cement was dry, and the fag packets and sweet wrappers among the dead leaves, and the other names carved into the seat, mark it out as teen territory. So today, although I want to go north towards Banbury, I am sitting on the chunky millennial bench on the Oxford side of the street. I shall cross when I see the bus coming.

The trouble is I'm so deep in my brown study of the map that I let the Banbury bus come and go without registering it; something in my brain simply edits it out because I'm on the wrong side. By now one or two Oxford-bound people have joined me, and seen me not catch it; and so when it comes out in chat that I'm planning on going the other way a slight wariness is manifest. They are more polite than the man in a tea-garden once in Devon where I was sitting with my pack — a little muddy and wild-haired possibly — and scoffing cream and scones and scribbling. He was quite likeably if rather Gradgrindishly teaching his children the birds that were coming to the feeder. 'Chaffinch, sparrow, great tit — and one flew over the cuckoo's nest', he finished with a sudden sneer, tipping his head in my direction.

I hadn't missed any buses that time, I was simply a lone, female walker: therefore, I must be mad. The man clearly hadn't read *One Flew Over the Cuckoo's Nest* or seen the film, or he would have known that maybe things are the reverse of his prejudice. Certainly I see walking as a good way to hold on to some sanity in a mad world. I suppose his attack — because he intended me to hear it — was provoked by what he perceived as a threat to his manhood. What would happen to him and his like if women no longer felt they needed his protection, and preferred their own company to his? Sadly, though he was an extreme example, the thing is very pervasive. Try an experiment. When out walking try asking some question of a male and female couple. How far is it to...? Is there a bridge further down? That sort of thing. And I guarantee that nine times out of ten it will be the man who answers. I try to subvert it by fixing the woman with my eye and ignoring the man, but usually he answers anyway. And when I'm out walking with Jeremy I do it too, I let him answer. He's better at map-reading, better at directions. But I'm working on it. And it's one of the reasons why, though I love him, I often choose to walk alone. There is a strength — I could almost believe there are muscles — that isn't physical, and I want to build it up.

The most depressing thing on this topic was a conversation I once had with an educated and apparently self-respecting expat Canadian woman. I think of Canadians, like Australians, as rugged and feisty, but obviously they vary. She told me that women *ought not* to walk alone, it was *asking for trouble.* Not just not unveiled or scantily clad, but not at all. She practises what she preaches, because in thirty-odd years I have never once seen her not actually hooked onto the arm of the necessary male. I think this is probably, rather literally, a personal hang-up, because when I did once walk alone in British Columbia, a wonderful wild trek through the trees and lakeshores of Buffy St. Marie's 'piney-woods home', I was not advised not to go, but only to be sure to wear a bear-bell, a small tinkling warning to let the bears know you are coming. Predatory humans never seemed to cross their minds. And to borrow a dog, as an additional bear-scarer and to get me back home if I got lost. I am not a dog owner or a dog lover, but I did, during the walk, come to love that particular dog, a black labrador called Mead. He must have covered at least twice the distance I did, because of his excited circlings into the woods. On the way back he waited for me at every turn in the track, and saw me safe home even when it was almost too dark to make out his faithful black shape. In this country you sometimes meet women walking in pairs, and sometimes on their own with a dog. Women completely alone are a rarer sight. One or two women have appeared on television supposedly doing it; but what of the hunky camera crew a few paces behind? So I never really know, with my moments of panic and my physical timidity, whether I am brave or cowardly.

It was tempting to omit the bus blunder. But then again it has the hallmark of puck on it, the brown-clad earth-spirit who delights in upsetting your plans — that is one of his attributes — and who is my metaphor for what I want from my walking. He sums it all up: I go out to meet him, and you can't choose how he manifests. So rather than wait an hour, I decide to go with the flow, and catch the bus going south. It's a beautiful day. I can walk where I like. I get off at the turning for Thrupp and walk down the lane to the canalside hamlet, which has a pub, a pretty terrace of trimmed-up cottages, and a beautiful eighteenth-century farmhouse. When I used to be parish clerk there, the farmer was chairman of the council, and meetings were sometimes held there. This wasn't good practice: a public meeting-place is less intimidating. And no members of the public ever did come to the meetings; but then maybe, in the late seventies, people were less community-minded anyway. Today on the parish notice board there is a schedule of Health Walks. Apparently they have leaders at the front and minders at the back and you can choose between walks of one, two or even three miles. You will need to sign a form though, first, for insurance purposes. I continue on my way feeling a good deal less feeble, indeed rather fit, and, uninsured and leaderless, a bit of risk-taker.

Glimpses of narrow-boat life appeal to our desire to get free into a simpler, slower, more real world. The full-timers tend to look more practical, and less self-consciously nautical. Their boats, with sacks of coal, tomatoes in grow-bags, and bikes on the roof, look — as they are — more lived-in. My son spent some years living on one, so I got to know the reality as well as the dream of life afloat. But what really stirs the buried longings in me are the couple of old cottages you come to when you've crossed the canal. You can just about see them from the end of their small, unspectacular gardens, with their small, old, fruit-trees. One can't stand around for too long prying into someone else's life — especially somehow a life that doesn't ask to be noticed or envied, only left alone — so I can't lurk pondering and trying to put my finger on what it is that is so lovely, and so unobtainable, and so nearly extinct. I sense it's something you can't replicate, something always lost in a too well-manicured, too carefully preserved village. You can't get it with money; but then money wouldn't want it anyway. It has to do with a life lived, probably over more than one generation, that involves contrivance, and seasonality, and it is not modern. It will probably die with the present occupants.

Under the railway and into a piece of 'community woodland': it's plain that people are hungry for a connection with the earth that doesn't just involve ripping it off. But the trees have been planted in dull blocks with dull straight grass paths between them, and I can't see how it can ever come to seem natural, even when a few more plants have colonised it. It will mellow a little perhaps, as even a perfunctory housing estate will when the brick has weathered and the roofs becomes mossy; but it is too regimented for beauty, unless perhaps when it falls into decay.

The difference as I emerge onto an old path is striking, because it runs diagonally uphill to the skyline, through a field which seems to have been left fallow and is full of wild flowers, with dandelion predominating and from which two larks are ascending. What will I see from the top? One of the pluses of having a poor memory is that I can still have that feeling on paths I've walked or books I've read before. What I see from the top of the rise is the path going on through ripe barley all the way to the trees and spire in Kidlington, and through it coming towards me are a granddad and two small boys with barley-coloured hair and bright red tops the colour of poppies, the little touch of red that completes the likeness to a Constable scene. As we cross the man is talking into a mobile phone, perhaps reporting back to his daughter. 'No, we didn't see no ducks', he says, 'but we saw the trains and was 'appy.' That's it really: that's what footpaths do, in a thousand small ways that are hard to put into legal language when we're called on to defend them —they make us 'appy.

As you cross over from old Kidlington, with its pretty stone houses snuggled close to that landmark steeple of St. Mary's, you come into the High Street and the less lovely church of the Baptists, which could pass for a primary school or the social security office. My dear generous old work-mate Mrs. B was a Methodist, and I remember once asking her the difference, and she pursed her lips in uncharacteristic reproof. 'Well you see there's no more room in the chariot, Mrs. T, that's what they believe.' Which may well be a travesty of some complex doctrine concerning predestination and the elect; though I share her abhorrence of exclusivity, especially when projected onto a supreme being. But the sun was shining and I was still feeling fit and enjoying my serendipitous walk, and something about the way the B of Baptist was hanging down made me feel they were only human, and probably didn't really believe that, not in their heart of hearts. Then I caught sight of some words low down on the side of the building that couldn't hang down because they were cut in stone THIS IS NONE OTHER THAN THE HOUSE OF GOD AND THIS IS THE GATE OF HEAVEN and they stood me still.

I've spent a lot of my life struggling with Christianity, half believing I couldn't be a good person without it, having enough intelligence to want to understand it, but never enough to see why suffering had needed to be built in. Finally I hope and believe I've left it behind, along with other troublesome things like periods and bus fares and being afraid of my mother. Sorry. It's hard not to be a little sharp and frivolous when one feels lightened of a load carried so long. Something of course remains. Vestiges. Long habits leave marks, like the lump on a middle finger where the pen rests. Or a slant, as a tree is skewed by a prevailing wind. And I hope the Sermon on the Mount *has* moulded me a little. You can tell I'm a touch de-mob happy but, though even recent history gives one every encouragement to give religion the thumbs-down, I'm trying not to overreact and become an earnest apostle of atheism. If anything could make me believe again it might well be Richard Dawkins tetchily telling me not to.

So when those words arrested me it wasn't with a call back to the fold, but with the power of language, of metaphor. The Authorised Version has more awe-power than any other on the market, and these people had the sense to know it. I could have laughed — did smile a bit — at the assurance that located the gate so precisely here. Though I realised they probably meant all Baptist churches... Or, to be fair, they may even have meant Here, or Wherever. The thing is, one has no power over the way people interpret stuff (I'm a writer, I know!) but whatever was intended, they'd laid the words on me and I was grateful, and went on my way uplifted, in the unpromising context of Kidlington High Street, a couple of hundred yards down the road from Tesco.

Back at the ranch I looked it up. Of course: Jacob's Dream. Should have remembered that — big-time affirmation, angels on the escalator, THE major awe-location. He was the guy who wanted blessing so badly that he blagged it. Because Jacob had issues, didn't he? Family issues, existential questions, like Who am I? Am I loved? and What's the point of it all? And stuff around wandering versus rootedness. And maybe he'd worked through some of them, maybe his psyche spoke and told him you're OK — it can happen — and he called it God and did at last feel blessed... Perhaps you have to give the files names or they don't get saved. It made sense that Jacob dreamed his dream out of doors, where he'd been sleeping rough with a stone for a pillow, lying on the earth. Then I half-recalled some lines of Francis Thompson and looked them up too:

> The angels keep their ancient places; -
> Turn but a stone, and start a wing!
> `Tis ye, `tis your estranged faces,
> That miss the many-splendoured thing.

And he continues with his image of Jacob's ladder 'pitched `twixt heaven and Charing Cross'— that's where my memory had been trying to lead me, through my untidy mind. For Charing Cross read Kidlington High Street. And for angels read…

Let me call some other witnesses. Robert Frost wondering how to explain to his neighbour his feeling that there was something that wanted walls to be dismantled. His friend Edward Thomas, walking through the Wiltshire countryside 'in search of something'. And for good measure Walt Whitman, who pegged the human condition as 'gross, hankering, mystical, nude'. 'Gross' needs to be understood in an old sense of fleshly, as Sebastian uses it in *Twelfth Night* when he says 'spirit I am indeed,/ But am in that dimension grossly clad'. Whitman saw us as both gross and mystical, body and spirit. When Public Enquiries are held into footpaths, witnesses are supposed to satisfy the powers that be that they are necessary. Necessities of the spirit are hard to speak about and harder still to prove: it doesn't mean they aren't real. In fact they are hidden in the word recreation. Ground is holy. We forget that over and over. Wherever you stand on the earth with the sky above you and feel like an earthling, that's the gate of heaven. As good a metaphor for feeling taken out of yourself and blessed and like you want in your gratitude to treat your neighbours and the planet with love and reverence as you can hope to find.

My uplifted mood carries me along the High Street past Tesco and the Co-op and a small row of old-fashioned shops, into The Black Bull, which already at five to eleven has four or five of those customers who look set for the day. It is a pub that got surrounded, a survival. The landlady is friendly and not too unworldly to stock my favourite apple-and-melon drink and even give me ice in it, and then leave me in peace. I sit contentedly for half an hour (I get the impression this is hasty by Black Bull standards) before strolling over to at last catch my bus going north. On a good day a quiet old-fashioned local has a good claim to being on the Way too. Ale, neighbourliness, time out. What more could you want? Gate of Heaven, has to be. None other.

Bus stop gossip says the small shops have all got to give way to a 'development'. If it's true I shall sorely miss the shop where you can buy single nuts and bolts and be served kindly and one-handedly by the lady of the shop as she breast-feeds her baby. We shall be yet another step closer to Huxley's Brave New World, where everything is as far as possible from the natural world.

When I ask for Rousham, the driver says, 'You'll have to tell me when, right?' It's clearly not a usual destination for bus folk, though you will usually find half a dozen middle-class, middle-aged cars parked in the grounds of the Big 'Ouse while their owners enjoy a peaceful stroll in its landscaped gardens. When my kids were small it was one of our great pleasures to spend the day there with a picnic. Every feature is part of their childhood: the sinuous rill which was perfect for small wellies to paddle along, the octagonal pool then mysteriously overhung with yews so that the water appeared blue, the steep lawns which could be rolled down, the strange grey-green nakedness and metallic drama of the statues, the lily pool with its huge red-golden fish, the bank of primroses below the William Kent arcade with its elegant curved and painted wooden eighteenth-century seats, the dark spidery tunnel down the middle of an old, thick, evergreen hedge. Even the carved praise of an otter-hound, which although we all deplored blood-sports was somehow likeable for its affection, and its evocation of a time when there *were* still otters in the Cherwell. And my own special delights — the thriving kitchen garden, the lovely herbaceous borders, and the dove-house with its turning wooden ladder and sweet stench in the dim interior. Then came a dark day when — so it is said — a Darren and some of his mates took it into their skin heads to break in and damage some of the statues. I presume they broke in, because it's hard to imagine their parents paying their entrance fee and then sitting there eating their sandwiches while it happened. In which case, breaking in remains an option. But whatever was the real reason, children under fifteen were officially banned from the garden from then on, and so my grandchildren are shut out of paradise.

Maybe it stops being heaven when some are excluded. Especially children. If you can't be like little children you can't get in, says the gospel. For years after that, even before I had grandchildren, I was too upset to go there; and when I did go back I found the trees gone from above the octagonal pool, and the lovely curved seats, presumably also victims of time, and so it seemed anyway a bit less like heaven than it had. But then I took an old friend whose sight was almost gone to sit under the trellis and smell the roses and listen to the fountain, and on another occasion one who grows amazing veg herself to enjoy and envy that Platonic ideal of a kitchen garden, which you approach, if you know the secret that I have discovered, through a wooden door in a wall hidden at the back of a grove. It is such a perfect way in, this hidden door, and the contrast so sharp between the treeish gloom behind you and the bright cultivated shelter of the walled garden, with its rows of artichokes, and chard, and asparagus, and flowers for cutting, such as sweet peas and dahlias, that I felt sure it must by now be locked. But it opened. Like the gate of heaven. And, if I'm completely honest, I kind of enjoyed the staid and placid atmosphere of the childless gardens, just as I relish the quiet coach on a Virgin train… If only they could have a children's day just once a week…

There is still something very special about Rousham. There is no gift shop or tea room, no notices. You are trusted to get your tickets from a machine, and I have never known anyone ask to see them. Unlike almost anywhere else in the country, you don't feel watched. Mysteriously, you hardly ever see anyone gardening, unless, occasionally, it is the lord or lady of the manor themselves. It can't all happen on a Monday — the one day it is closed to the public. When I see the place from a distance, perhaps from the rise to the north where the 'eye-catcher' is — a pretend ruin placed there to be seen from the garden — I feel included, because I know what is inside those park walls so well.

On the other hand, in the parish of Rousham, only one public footpath remains. In Tackley, the (admittedly larger) next parish to the south, there are a couple of dozen. A path which was used within living memory to connect the two parishes was closed in the 1950s, when I suppose people were less on the ball. So I set off up the one path with mixed feelings. On the one hand, with my mental map of the landscape gardens, having a sense of belonging. On the other, walking this single, somehow begrudging and obviously little-used path, which isn't even signposted as it should be, feeling like an intruder, though I am quite within my rights. It makes a gentle uphill diagonal through ridge-and-furrowed pasture which thankfully, since the Rousham herd are beautiful chestnut but nevertheless heavily-built longhorns, is at present empty. It heads towards a wood, Dean Plantation, somewhere beyond which I can hear a buzzard mewing.

There is a pleasant breeze and the sun is shining on the great gold ingots of bales on a cut field up to the horizon to the northeast. Following the map, because the line of the path is not visible on the ground, I keep left of a small enclosed group of trees. It looks as though they might conceal a spring. Such features, providing variety and beauty, but also suggesting a tolerance and accommodation between agriculture and nature, are agreeable to the spirit as well as to the eye. A line of fine mature chestnuts meets the fence at the corner by the stile, and then you are into the wood, and suddenly, mysteriously, on a visible path — who makes it? A string of young pheasants run ahead of me, but it can hardly be them; and a muntjac crosses the path, a branch of which goes steeply downhill for a few yards to a fast and busy B road, and straight over it into another parish and another pasture.

This one is full of lively cream-coloured bullocks that gallop round me, as in a rodeo. Oxfordshire is one of those counties that has a 'cow clause'. This means that the farmer is allowed to run a bull on a footpath, provided that it is in with cows. The opportunity for the beast to satisfy his lusts is supposed to make him less dangerous, but many people with better country-cred than mine will tell you not to trust one under any circumstances, and so, always anxious about one thing or another, I am in the habit of scanning the herd before I enter the field, to check if a bull is present, and to give him a wide berth. Otherwise, to the admiration of townee friends, I pride myself on being able to deal with cattle; but when I hoosh these away, with as confident a manner as I can muster, they back off exaggeratedly and immediately return. There's a very miry patch on my route, much poached by hooves, and one of my boots gets temporarily stuck in the dark slough, and then there's a steep uphill out of it, so I reach the stile breathless, pursued by a single bullock practising for being a bull, who keeps on after me when the rest have lost interest. I climb with some difficulty into a narrow band of scrubby wood on an awkward slope, ducking under sloes and dodging brambles, while trying to keep enough momentum to not slip back, and escape out into a cut field which today has a kestrel hanging above it and rooks gleaning in it, and scarlet pimpernel in flower among the stubble.

On the far side you come by this back way into the village of Steeple Aston, past a hedge of fat-hipped roses which today is full of sparrows and greenfinches. The path continues across the road as a mown alley, and then, obviously well-used, through a small old green paddock that feels like the peaceful heart of the village, with a soothing sound-track of woodpigeons, to a metal kissing-gate. Beyond this it runs between stone walls, but low enough to give you a good view of a whimsical and slightly neglected water garden, involving tin-can waterwheels and pleasantly amateur wooden sculptures. The people of Steeple will be familiar with this garden and its maker, but it is striking to an outsider. It is more Heath Robinson than Ian Hamilton Finlay, but someone has obviously enjoyed constructing this, and their pleasure communicates itself. It's a long garden, with the water at the bottom, and further up are some of the tallest sunflowers I can remember seeing — they look to be twelve feet at least — and runner beans and potatoes, and apples ripening, and chickens and gladioli and dahlias and snapdragons. From over the wall on the other side floats a nostalgic garden flower scent. I stand inhaling for a while, but can't place it. Gardens are paradises, people's visions attempted, over-egged, neglected, given up on, or radiantly realised. And so, to some extent and more constrained by income, are their houses. Walking by them you can catch a whiff of what other people have longed for, usually by signs and tokens rather than by the achieved whole. A house-name, a sociable party of gnomes, a wigwam of old-fashioned, spicy sweet peas, a Fragonard swing on a tree. If we are postulants of heaven then let's hope that, as the universities always claim, they are looking for potential, and it doesn't so much matter what schooling life has brought you.

I take a path out of the village that has a pretty border of wild oats, poppies, and a dainty white umbel I never seem to be able to identify. These are the wild flowers that escaped the spray by being at the very edge, a reminder of what fields used to look like. My ex-husband used to refer appreciatively to 'Nature's herbaceous border', and he was right — there is a beauty to the chance juxtapositions that you'd be hard put to reproduce deliberately. After a while there's a patch of woodland, Three Corner Clump, and I sit on a fallen larch to eat my lunch, with green woodpeckers making their witches' cackle somewhere close at hand. Another woman parks her car at the entrance to the track and with her two dogs and her stick limps a short constitutional round the wood. On the road into Middle Aston the lake is hidden by dense planting of quick-growing evergreens. It is in such a different spirit from the low-walled little water-garden in Steeple, and even from Rousham House. There is one gap, with a gate, and I veer towards it, to have my spirits refreshed by the sight of water, only to find a notice telling me to *Keep Out, Rotweiler On Guard*, which puts me off even from pausing to look. The hostility extinguishes what the view might otherwise offer. And it's pure chav. Let's face it, brash metal notices and rotweilers are *vulgar*, apart from being out of place in heaven. This is obviously the gate to somewhere else.

Rightly looked at, all ground is holy. Not as in, Keep Out, this belongs to our religion, but as in, This is a patch of the earth's surface that has its own special qualities, that may be home to something even if it's only a bunch of beetles, and so can be visited and investigated and enjoyed in a peaceful manner leading to love, and is an unsuitable place to do bad things in.

PRIVATE PARTS

Deddington hopes for tourists. An inviting leaflet publicises its history and beauties, and how to get to it by road, rail, or even, improbably, by air. Take a traveller's tip though, and pee before you arrive — there are no public loos. The coffee shop was suggested, but turned out to be closed on Tuesdays (or whenever) and naturally this was a Tuesday (or whenever). It seemed a bit early for a pub, so I headed out of town sharpish. The path I wanted, the path to the Mill, heads north off the Hempton Road. But which road through the housing development would luxuriously downshift into a bridlepath?

Highway authorities have a duty to signpost paths where they leave a metalled road, which is meant to be helpful, and usually is, but in this kind of situation leaves you guessing because the signpost is hidden further in. First turning, Gaveston Gardens. Curious name. Later. Mustn't waste urgent minutes getting it wrong down cul-de-sac. Young man! Young man friendly but has never heard of Mill, a mile away, and regards map regretfully as foreign script. Banish time-wasting thoughts about what I would do if made Minister for Education. Risk second turning, The Daedings. What are daedings? Later. Speed-walking, I come to a merciful signpost — Bridlepath to Daeda's Wood, what's that? it's not on the map — and plunge on — yes! on a path now — between houses and a pretty disorder of garden-escaped buddleias and hollyhocks, onto a wide stony track with an old hedge, goaded by the sound of running water in the ditch alongside, until at last I'm able to step off into a leafy privy out of sight of back windows.

What I needed of course was a *Philips Street Atlas*, which my daughter has since equipped me with. It doesn't sound like what a country walker needs. Streets? That's what you're getting away from, isn't it? But getting away, out of a town or a village, is often the difficult bit. And it set me thinking about streets, and history, and names. Like Gaveston. I knew a Gaveston from Marlowe's *Edward II*, not a very admirable character, as I recalled; Piers Gaveston, gay gold-digger of the thirteenth century who makes today's cash for peerages seem like very small beer. Marlowe has Edward create him Lord High Chamberlain, Earl of Cornwall and King and Lord of Man, and that's just in the first scene. Not a lot of time for the public either: 'As for the multitude, they are but sparks,' he decides, 'Raked up in embers of their poverty.' It turns out it is that Gaveston: he spent a short time in Deddington in 1312, waiting to be executed. Gaveston Gardens has a posh ring to it, you'd guess at a postcode in Belgravia; yet if anyone's life was a warning against pretension it was his. The King's favourite: it has a cheerful, sporting sound. Maybe they thought he was a horse. Or maybe they weren't that fussy. Like the minor public school in Wodehouse which welcomed 'anything in spats' to address them on Speech Day, maybe a minor market town will settle for anything in spurs. The Daedings, too, is a grab for history. Daeda gave his name to the whole town, so it's a major roots bid: we go way back — early Saxon — that's as far back, in these parts, as it goes. And Daeda's Wood, too new to be on the maps, represents a millennial determination to buck the trend and do something lasting and lovely.

The track leads downhill off the ridge, alongside an old hedge of tall oaks and ashes. Beyond on either hand the wheat is ripe. There's a late snatch of blackcap's song, and a bolt of white rump into the hedge, followed by the weak pipe that equals bullfinch. Also I identify whitethroat and dunnock: I'm getting better at the LBJs. (Stands for Little Brown Job: hard for the novice to distinguish.) That phrase 'the whitethroat builds' in *Home Thoughts from Abroad* seems so impressive.

Was Browning a keen birder or were whitethroats more plentiful in his day? The brook has somehow got itself over the other side of the track, and there are tiny skaters on the surface. Polleny yellowhammers everywhere. We emerge, the track and I, onto a lane with a pheasant on it. A green woodpecker calls from an oak.

A few yards down this narrow lane to the left are two large identical notices, one on either side: THERE IS NO RIGHT OF WAY THROUGH DEDDINGTON MILL. THIS PATH WAS EXTINGUISHED IN THE 1960s. I am intrigued by the overkill. If people are still presenting themselves in numbers after forty years and demanding to go through, it suggests it was a well-known path, a nice place to walk, a sensible through route. Short of mass trespasses, surely the Council is going beyond the call of duty here? It would be nice if they sometimes did so on the positive side, since doubt often turns us back. They could make notices, for paths that have not yet legally been put to death, that would say things like YOU HAVE A PERFECT RIGHT TO WALK THROUGH HERE (despite the barbed wire, locked gate, fierce dog). IT HAS BEEN A PATH SINCE THE YEAR DOT. As a matter of fact I was once involved in trying to save this path, though I'm pretty sure it was in the '70s. You had to find people who would testify that they had walked it unchallenged for twenty years or more. I did find one, an elderly man who wasn't deaf, had all his marbles, and seemed unlikely to be intimidated. Excellent! 'And would you be willing to give evidence?' He wouldn't. 'I'll be dead soon, and I don't care what happens after that.' In vain my talk of grandchildren, of future generations: he was childless, and heavy-souled. And so now the path, like him, is extinguished, spark gone out.

Sometimes though the multitude strikes back. Turn right on that narrow lane, and here is a notice put up in a very different spirit. WELCOME, it says. You are welcome to walk here at any time. A project of the Woodland Trust and the local community, Daeda's Wood is young and beautiful and full of hope, a baby named after its doughty great great grandfather. In bloom in clearings between the trees are vetches, cranesbills, knapweeds, campions, poppies, yarrow. For starters. The small sinuous River Swere runs through, and you can stand at an opening on the bank above a bend and a bunch of writhen sycamore roots, and contemplate the water, and the yellow water lilies. Snails are out and about: our new path has crossed their terrain. No-one else is around, but by the bench where you can sit and listen to the river, and the birds, there's a fag end and some fresh strawberry hulls. What do you make of that, Holmes? I should say it means it's a good place to be, Watson.

Out the other side, on another narrow road, with grass breaking through it and orange molehills on its verge, a driver waves and smiles in a way that says, Boy, are you doing the right thing! I am his snail on the thorn. Near Bloxham Bridge is an extinguished weasel, frozen in its speedy, fierce curve. At the top of the rise of Coombe Hill you can turn and look back over a big sweep of country — trees, fields, and whitey-grey clouds. Middle English country. We'll dig in over there, says Daeda, on that next ridge. But then I'm plucked abruptly from my Dark Age reverie by yet another notice: SURVEILLANCE CAMERAS. Flytipping an offence. Fine of £50,000. And/or prison. *What??* Also, why? And who? I wasn't expecting wilderness when I came out here: Daeda put paid to that in nine-something. But I was expecting 'to get away from it all'. Why would anyone bring their junk out here? If they were minded to hire a van and drive their so last year's three-piece suite somewhere, why not to the tip? And that it should have happened enough times for surveillance cameras to seem like the only answer… I glance about nervously. Am I infringing anything? Was I picking my nose? I can't see any cameras, but maybe they're disguised as sheep or something, like with David Attenborough. Voyeurism is clearly pretty widespread these days, though this hardly seems a choice site. I've not so far watched Big Brother, and felt no urge to; though I know a lot of people do, maybe even the multitude. But I am curious, about lots of stuff. I'm always on the hoof, grazing, gleaning, an eager snapper-up of unconsidered trifles of observation. So why do I feel these cameras are bad form? It seems unsporting I suppose, like trawling in a fly-fishing place.

Yet *another* notice explains that we musn't use the path that looks like and obviously is a path, through a gate, direct and avoiding farm buildings, but must follow signs through the yard. This too is weird: usually farmers like to keep walkers at arm's length. I'm so unnerved by now I almost turn back to seek the sanctuary of Daeda's Wood, where I am welcome, welcome to walk at any time. What a lovely word that is. But

I summon my small allowance of dogless courage by thinking of my venturesome daughter walking alone in foreign parts, and of my granddaughter for whom I want the world to lie open as much as for my grandson. In the event, there are no fierce dogs or farmers; in fact no-one seems to live there at all. The yard is eerily empty as I obediently follow the waymarks to exit with relief onto the track, a hundred yards from the gate through which I could so much more easily and less intrusively have entered upon it. It leads downhill, wide, stony and unfenced, through sheep pasture showing the old ridge-and-furrow patterns. There is always a yellowhammer somewhere in earshot or in view. Down by the exaggerated meanders of the Swere, cutting into the grass like an interlocking jigsaw, there are bales of hay in black plastic with a good, fruity scent leaking out, and an old wooden shepherd's hut on wheels, derelict and with rusty metal patches. It might perhaps have been new in Hardy's day: it certainly speaks of Hardy's world. I come to a midden with its dark seepings, and a pretty stone mill house, again empty.

Here the path I need turns off the main track and crosses a small paddock-field in which are two frisky chestnut horses. It pays to be wary of horses, so I stand on the stile sussing out the route, and then cross smartly and straight, as at a zebra crossing. On the far side are a pair of stiles where you cross the Swere, and the remains of the shapely, handcut stonework of an earlier bridge. The next field has sheep in long rough grass, and I follow a path through it for a while before realising it's the sheep that have made it; though it proves to be more or less on the right line. Swallows swoop low for the insects that accompany animals and dung. Out once more into Snakeshill Lane, a wide, cindery track leading uphill to the hamlet of Hempton. To one side of it a great ploughed field is dotted with white and black, gulls and rooks. Paths lead off to either side, but while one is clearly visible, leading temptingly over the skyline, the other has been ploughed out. I guess that the reason for this is that one has been designated as part of the 'Deddington Circular Walk' and the other not. It confirms what's sometimes said that marketing walking in this way leads to the overuse of particular paths and the neglect of others. But it seems better that at least some paths are looked after and used, and new people introduced to the pleasures of walking them, than that the whole network is ignored and overgrown or obstructed. Until we have the Swedish right to roam in all reasonable places, all measures to maintain our existing rights have to be a good thing.

Under the tall ashes and sycamores that shade the track as it enters Hempton is, you've guessed it, a notice. This one says that the land to one side is 'residential garden' and that no public right of way exists. There's no sign of a path, and without the notice I would have enjoyed the glimpses of paradisal slopes and passed on untroubled. But now the Leveller in me demands, When is a garden not a garden? and answers, When it's too big! Too big is, obviously, bigger than ours. When we got back late one night to find an alien car parked and three strangers having some kind of orgy in our garden, we did not say Friends, feel free! We saw them off and cursed modern youth and next day went grimly out in rubber gloves to deal with the cans and spliff-ends and condoms, like the castle-dwelling Englishmen we are. Why couldn't they have gone a couple of hundred yards further down the lane to the sewage works? That always used to be the Friday and Saturday night-spot. Though we did several times get knocked up by shame-faced shaggers who wanted help to get their car out of the ditch… But though I too want my privacy, my bit of uninvaded space, I can't but recognise the buried longing that brings people out into the country for their ill-judged idylls. It isn't new. In the '60s my in-laws, who lived on the edge of a Kentish wood, used to click their tongues over the people who came to use the clearing they quaintly referred to as 'the Motor-car Grass'. In Shakespeare's day people fooled about 'between the acres of the rye'. And I daresay Daeda couldn't move for coupling couples; but at least they didn't arrive by car. Or scatter condoms. A huge warren in a sandy bank cheers me up: rabbits are truly communal, and they take their pleasures freely in our gardens.

A Hempton house is being faced with thin pieces of orange stone over breeze blocks. I feel somehow embarrassed, as though I had caught it in its underwear. All is appearance and surface. Though it's no secret. Beauty is plastic surgery. Even the ads acknowledge it: your hair need only be healthy-*looking*. Nearby a house called Stonewalls has those very walls patched with concrete, and an electronic gate, and a warning about the dog. Four young people with dyed hair and black clothes — in short, not 'ramblers' — have walked out here along the road. They ask me where the nearest pub is and are disappointed when I tell them it's back in

Deddington. They're out here for the country and don't quite know how to access it. There are moments when I'm not sure either. Even the church is shut. Nevertheless I sit gratefully on the seat outside it to eat my lunch, although being sharply un-bumshaped it too is clearly for appearance only. I'm curious about this guarded, publess place, and take a little loop of footpath round the back of it, called Old Plough Walk. This feels more accommodating, and smells of pineapple weed, and I pass the time of day with a young woman and her two kids and two dogs, peacefully idling there to take the air behind the gardens, which can be glimpsed over an absurd wavy fence presumably designed to express that this is the country.

On my way back beneath the chestnut avenue that lines the road, a branch just misses me, and I look up thinking, Boys! But no, it was just the tree moulting, and the next day I read a piece in the paper about how trees in this drought are dropping apparently healthy branches. There are boys though, further on, two boys of about fourteen lying and resting and drinking pop beside their bikes, without an electronic game in sight, and who return my greeting pleasantly. A good old-fashioned sight to my grandmotherly heart, except that — which makes it even better — one of them is Asian.

I turn off onto a tarmacked track which a black beetle is crossing, and which is decorated with bird droppings looking like blackcurrants and cream. Wind sounds in the wheat. At Tomwell Farm I'm again being watched, images of me, 'for crime prevention and public safety'. On reading that I feel suddenly less safe, though by now I'm getting inured to the paranoia. I suppose being surveilled is better than being torn apart by guard dogs. I take a grassy track through wheat, which soon becomes rougher. Deddington church tower with its golden weathercocks is now in sight again. A red admiral leads the way. The map calls this Plumdon Lane, but it appears to be scarcely used. This broad green lane between tall old apple-trees, oaks and ashes was clearly more of a thoroughfare at one time, but I can't think many criminals or members of the public needing to be saved from them pass this way now. Green rose-hips make me think that I must remember to come here again in June, when it will be even more beautiful, hung with pink and white hedge roses and their scent. *Hoo-wheet*, the call of a young chiffchaff, and a snatch of blackbird's song. A huge fallen tree blocks the exit onto the main road, but it can be got round, and I walk the short distance back up into town, passing, even on the verge of the trafficky main road where you don't want to linger, a magnificent stand of orange lords-and-ladies.

In the square, which is away from the main road, I sit outside a pub with a pot of tea. Inside, it is one of those places where teens hang out, wanting, in the perverse way of adolescence, to be in the dark on a fine day. Someone from my own village happens by, and we are pleased to see one another, but have that sort of embarrassed, surprised encounter of people out of context.

FOOTNOTES

From the bus I catch sight of a shrunken old man. He is bent over but bright-eyed and alert to the life out of doors. It is far more interesting to him than the tele — enlivens two more senses at least, and it has an air, a current, a spark. On board too we are a lively bunch. There are teens in the back with their bare bits and their feet tucked up and their lifeline music machines. 'This is still number one of my Most Played...I've played it like, fifty times?' I warm to her. I'm a bit of an obsessive myself, over tracks of both kinds. When I was a teen like her I had an EP of Kid Ory's Creole Jazz Band, which may even have contributed to my craze for walking. They were playing *Walkin' to New Orleans*, and I can still hear it in my head though the vinyl got bent and busted years ago. Apart from the teens, there's a woman with a toddler and a pushchair and a staggering number of carrier bags, looking like the carbon quota for an entire village, that have to be passed out to her when she gets off. But at least she is using the bus.

In Middle Barton after a search I locate the bridlepath I want — it is one of those that now exit the back of an estate when it must once have plunged straight into the fields. 'Keep to the footpath, stay out of the grass,' a notice adjures me, adding 'Thank you' and softening the tone.

I unlatch the metal gate and it drops heavily on its hinge, suggesting it's not often used. I manage to get it back up, and proceed up the grass track beside a tall hedge that contains purple elderberries and green, yellow and red haws in different stages of ripeness. I pass a big gout of dusty dark fur — badger? The other day I saw some canisters I didn't at all like the look of near the entrances to our local sett… It has been explained, with evidence, that gassing them only makes the problem worse, that the escapees will move off and, if they are infected with tuberculosis, pass it on to the next patch. But there is a kind of thwarted housewife mentality that sometimes seems to come into play among tough men. They like to clean up. They are always tidying. One thinks of the exterminations of street kids in parts of South America, as though they were bluebottles or roaches.

The yellow flowers of St John's wort. A meadow brown butterfly. The next gate is not locked but has a rusty loop of wire that I can't budge, so I climb it. A small flock of birds flies off piping, in a close, undulant group. I wish I could learn to identify more surely, but I enjoy their proximate life even though I can't name them. *Hooweet!* sounds from the hedge — now that I can identify: chiffchaff. Someone once described to me his great pleasure in the acquisition of bird songs and calls, how he now walked through the countryside surrounded by unseen friends. His words stayed with me, and with each new song or call learned I have life that much more abundantly.

There's a small, newish plantation next, in which are guelder roses, oaks, ashes, dogwoods. In a decade it will be a wood. We are coming round to woods again, and planting for the future. There was a time when the frilled rings on an architect's plan were sometimes little more than artistic licence. Regarding which you have to keep your wits about you. Cheered by the picture of piled logs beside it in the catalogue, I once almost chose that particular stove. Could I occasionally burn anthracite nuts as well, if I had 'flu say, and had run out? What? Oh, you can't burn *wood* on it, that's not advised at all. Close one! Supposing I hadn't happened to ask? I referred them to the picture, but they could see no connection. And, to do them a kind of justice, I have since seen artistic piles of actual logs in pubs that have neither fireplaces nor chimneys. Logs are symbols of a past where life was more real and rural, in the same category as haystacks and cows called

Buttercup without tags on their ears. The tide is turning though. 'Wood-burning stoves' are being asked for and supplied. Suddenly I am not the only person round here with my eye on the dead elms — the trouble is, the others have power saws, which I consider unsporting. A local pub charts the progress from rural to genteel to green — it used to be called *The Dog*. Then it had a makeover and suddenly it was *The Squire Bassett*. And then about a year ago they took and painted it what my mother would have called *eau de nil* and it is now, mysteriously, *The Dogwood*, and the local eco-group has its meetings in there.

The track I'm on — to get back to it — has some old metalling of stones, suggesting that like a lot of the bridleways round here it was once a route of more significance. It is prettily bordered with white camomile and the hedge is full of the red berries of honeysuckle, contrasting with these Platonic ideals of blackberries, ripe but not overripe and of a good size. I realise joyfully that my now empty lunch box is the perfect receptacle and in no time I pick enough for our supper. And, as I set off again, there on the path is a sealed, damp, white envelope, on which is written 'Harriet Hunter' (this is her pen name) 'One horse'. Inside are twenty pounds. I pocket my find and step onward more quickly, no longer an ambler but a detective with a case to solve. The bridleway gives onto a minor road, which I head along in light rain until I come to a farm. The door stands open in the easygoing but now less common country way, and I call out, but there's no reply. Further into the yard is a curly-haired stable lad with a taking smile, a young puck if ever there was one. Messing about with horses is a regular puckish occupation. He listens in a friendly way while I ask if he knows of a Harriet Hunter hereabouts who also has to do with horses, but I can't make out his answer. I hesitate embarrassedly, and 'I'm *Irish*,' he says, grinning more than ever, and suddenly, as though he had magicked my ears to understand Faery, I can comprehend him perfectly well. It's an odd phenomenon that. I can remember struggling with a fat, turgid-seeming book of literary criticism when I was at college. It was one of those where you keep having to start a sentence again from the beginning and take another run at it. To start over, as they say in the States. It was in fact written by an American, and when I suddenly hit on the idea of reading it inside my head with an American accent, all was plain. Well, plainer.

The puck directed me to another farm nearby where a lady called Harriet lived. He didn't know her other name but he knew she kept horses. It had to be her. It's come on to rain harder by now, and as I turn damply into the rather posh drive I am trying to remind myself that I am not a vagrant or a footpad but a respectable middle-class woman on a highly respectable errand — returning lost property. No dogs attack me and no-one asks *Can I help you?* in that tone that means the opposite. But the young people who are gardening in an efficient and motorised sort of a way shake their heads. Wrong Harriet. Never heard of Harriet Hunter. They direct me pleasantly back to the village by footpath: 'You can cut through here to it.'

Back in Middle Barton I head for the pub. Absurd though it seems I am almost breathless with the excitement of the case, or chase, and with wanting to crack it before the last bus comes. My old friend Lorrie Dowsett, who years ago ran the Youth Hostel at Littledown Farm near Milton Abbas in Dorset, would have known how I felt. His hostel had no electricity but was well-supplied with goat's milk. The smell of the billy mixed with lamp-oil was the smell of his welcoming small farm, isolated, up a steep track about a mile from the road. In winter, when the hostel was closed, he wrote books, which he would then print on his own small, labour-intensive press. (Naturally, the hostel was closed altogether before long: 'Not up to the standards of modern hostellers' or some such phrase.) The books were called *The Youth Hostel Mysteries* and featured a private eye by the name of John Masters, and were billed as 'for anyone who enjoys mystery but dislikes murder and crime'. The puzzles were always in a rural setting and involved a lot of legwork: I felt I'd stepped into one. Lorrie was a big man and completely bald from some prehistoric form of radiotherapy which he had survived. He could seem an alarming presence. In fact, he was the gentlest man alive. He died last year, aged over ninety, mourned by his family and a small band of hostellers as eccentric as himself; and so the gentlest man alive is now someone else, probably my partner Jeremy, and another true original is gone. In a world of imitation I can ill spare the real.

The lad in charge of The Carpenter's Arms — which is cheeringly open, mid-week, mid-afternoon and with one solitary customer — seems way too young for the job, though that may be a side-effect of my cronedom (doctors, policeman, politicians all seem too young, so why not barmen?). The only customer, who seems to be a mate of his, clocks my urgent on-the-case manner when I say I have found something. 'Is it a body?' he asks. They haven't heard of Harriet Hunter either, but they lend me the phone book. There are two or three possible entries, but the most likely is at yet another farm, in Duns Tew. I stride off again and try it from the phone box, but there's no reply. Not having a sergeant or a side-kick I decide to clock off for the day, and have just time before the bus to go back to the pub for a drink and to report progress. The barboy is on his own again and talks heart-warmingly about how happy he is to live here. A couple of years ago he and his mum had lived in Blackbird Leys. It sounds lovely but is one of those poignant misnomers that speak of our longings and society's betrayals, being — whatever it once was — a notoriously rough estate on the outskirts of Oxford. He still seems to relish the delight of relocation freshly, and grimaces a bit fearfully at the memory of the family they lived next door to — 'one of the bad ones'. 'And now,' he says gratefully, gesturing out towards rural peace and greenness and a slower pace, 'we have all this...'

A week or two later, on a different walk, I finished up at Middle Barton again. The mingled sounds of music and football cheers met me on the road, and I found I'd coincided with the church fête. A cup of tea! Homemeade cake! Never mind that the playing field shelter was heavily graffitied by THE BOYZ, who were present themselves in some numbers watching the game, it was an innocent, festive occasion. The odd posh lady peddled plants, and the smiling vicar in cream linen could have been straight out of *Midsomer Murders*, but they were misleading. It was altogether more downmarket than that and much more interesting. A tractor and trailer advertising the Banbury and District Ploughing Competition is giving small circular rides to eight or ten children at a time. Normally my best tombola win is a tin of beans, but there's a kind of luck sometimes comes with being a stranger, and soon I'm stuffing a bottle of Chardonnay into my pack, *and* an aromatherapy set. Best of all is a hardback copy of *The Crossing* by Cormac McCarthy, whose close-to-the-bone writing about lives lived close to the earth I had serendipitously discovered in a holiday cottage just recently, among the usual whodunnits and novels past their sell-bys. Exciting, live writing.

Why hadn't anyone told me about him? And here, now, on this unlikely bookstall, was another. My goose-bumps tell me it was intended for me, but of course I don't believe that, do I? Sometimes, especially when in receptive, appreciative mood, one just strikes lucky...

I took in also the little twelfth-century church of Edward the Confessor where there was a small and very beautiful flower festival, and looked at photographs of the countryside around and read how Sonia Norgrove had walked thirty-seven miles of it in fifteen hours and ten minutes and raised £815 for a rehab centre for the paralysed in Bangladesh. Sharing her luck in being able to walk, and at living in a (so far) temperate zone.

On the present occasion I catch the bus home and make a phone call, and very much astonish Harriet with the news that I have her money. I think she too feels a bit superstitious and lucky. Her Mum is there to meet the bus next morning and is full of thanks and wonder. (I hope she will think better of ramblers in the future, and spread the word to other farmers...) The wonder is for my honesty, and also that I'm walking on my own 'without even a dog for company'. She's a feisty farmer's wife, but obviously thinks I have bottle, so I'm back thinking maybe I'm braver than I feel. I don't reveal that dogs are what worry me most, and when we've parted ways and I head down a path in the direction of North Aston, telling myself I'm intrepid, and the first dog of the day comes barking up it towards me, it's a breeze. And the owner panting behind instead of telling me it's the fault of my hat, pack, boots, coat, or stick, or that I should have walked on or stood still or had a dog of my own, all which have been offered as excuses for my being harassed, apologises. It's soon clear that he regularly takes the dog a short way down the slippery, ochreous path beside the crop for its comfort break and doesn't expect to meet anyone else, because after a short way the dog turds give out and so does any sign of the path. I continue on the same line, gently downhill, and by and by the crop changes from corn to black beans with a cheerful invasion of tall yellow flowers, and here I'm able at least to follow a tractor line more or less on the route. The corner by the brook has thick willows, and hazels with whitey-brown nuts, and numbers of tits, finches and blackbirds flitting in and out of them. My friend Jean first introduced me to the phrase 'a feeding party', at which I laughed, as being altogether too Little Grey Rabbit. But I've since realised that it is, of course, perfectly scientific: numbers of small birds of different species will often congregate where there's a mutually agreeable source of food. The next field is sweet and warm with red clover, and there is even a waymark on the footbridge, though I struggle to get through the brambles and nettles that are growing over it.

These are footnotes, and footnotes don't fit in. The function of a footnote is to move things not considered to be properly a part of the main text out of the way. We must above all be able to screech down the autobahn unhindered. What goes into a footnote varies from a simple acknowledgement of a source — a chapter and verse thing — all the way to pages and pages from another book — the one the writer suddenly wishes she were writing instead of the present one. Sometimes a footnote goes off at a tangent; sometimes it goes into something more deeply. Sometimes it's packed with research; sometimes a mere jeu d'esprit. It can gloss a word or a fact that time or a different culture has rendered obscure. All these properties it shares with the ambler's experience of the world, which is grateful and explorative and curious; and like that experience it is considered secondary, squeezed into small print, and skipped altogether by mainstreamers in a hurry to get somewhere.

Crossing the fast main road is a reminder of the other world — the real world or the false one, depending on your view. I then have to walk along it, pathless, for almost half a mile, my ears, nose and thoughts under assault, my being tense and concentrated on getting through this bit fast and in one piece; and I turn thankfully, though with a different kind of trepidation, into the drive of Daneshill Farm. The name turns out to have a certain irony: there are pigs! So many of the local pig farmers have given up, unable to compete with the Danes; and here not only are there pigs out in the open, but they are delightfully spotted and various, clearly one or some of the old breeds. The farmer asks me if I know where I am going, but quite pleasantly, and I say North Aston, and we agree together on where the path goes. There are some beautiful mature trees beside the house, and an ancient feel to the place. I don't like to stand around for too long gawping at the man's home, but I try to tuck it into my mind like a nun adding someone to her prayer list. It seems like a small island. I hope the ocean of modernity won't rise and cover it.

The path crosses rough pasture, steeply down and up again, with the backs of North Aston houses at the far side of the view. There is even a slight visible trace of it, so I'm not the only person to pass this way in historical times. At North Aston there is a little local difficulty: the right of way passes through a garden, but the stile is blocked by a huge roll of wire, and when I somehow get over it I step into a ditch full of water, up to my knees. A notice tells me also to Beware of the Dog. I can't face the dog or its owner, so I half straddle the ditch and half wade a few yards along to a bridle gate that opens easily and sneak out that way, which was probably the idea all along. And I could have gone straight out of the field that way. Round the front of the house is a footpath sign accompanied by another dog warning. Whether or not there really is a dog, this is still illegal: you are not supposed to keep a dangerous animal on a footpath, nor to put up what is known in law as a 'misleading notice', to try to discourage people from exercising their rights. It would be better all round if the path could be officially diverted through the gate, but it may involve someone else's land, and in any case would provide work for lawyers and bureaucrats, and most of us don't want that. Instead of the hostile and illegal notices however, how about 'It's easier this way and nobody minds' and a friendly little hand pointing, like on the internet? It would spread a different spirit and probably guard their privacy better. And their health. Being angry full time is really bad for the blood pressure.

The lane to Steeple Aston passes what used to be pig sheds and is now an antiques place. There have been so many changes in the forty years that I've lived in this part of Oxfordshire that I feel a bit of an antique myself, a quaint old thing whose use has been forgotten or superseded, but like which they don't make 'em any more… The two most painful to me were the uprooting of one of a double line of willows, and the end of the Woodstock bakery. I stood and pleaded with the farm manager, but he said modern machines couldn't get along the ditch to dredge it. The thwarted housewifery again: nature is so untidy. To me of course it was a stream and not a ditch. He said I was sentimental for a time when men with shovels did the job. In fact neither man nor machine has cleared it since and it remains a stream, with yellow flags and forget-menots, an occasional kingfisher route, so he might just as well have let the trees stay. This happened at the peak of the time of pulling hedges out and making huge prairie fields. Thankfully now there is some replanting.

As for the baker, he was straight out of the Happy Families pack — round, red, cheerful and possibly even (though this may be my imagination filling in) floury. His name was Mr.Wiggins, and he would come to the door with a basket on his arm containing a selection of lovely, fresh, crusty bread. One day he came with the longest face, a shocking thing in itself, so that we immediately asked him what was the matter. 'They're closing me down,' he said. 'They say my ovens are not up to modern standards.' Like the hostels. If I could ever identify these modern people who were so foolishly exacting I would argue with them, but I never found anyone who was anything but very sad about the bakery. And the hostel, for that matter: and in any case, no-one forced people who wanted to arrive by car and have tele and en suite to stay there. A few serious questions are finally being asked about the true healthfulness of 'modern standards', but it's too late for Littledown Farm, and for Mr.Wiggins.

I digress. (Yeah! Waytogo!) I reach home as a huge electric storm begins — thunder, lightning, hail, followed by lashings of slanty rain. I am seriously glad not to be out in that; I feel quite looked after. I rush round shutting windows. The frames are of old, thick, hard wood, painted and repainted. They certainly don't make 'em like *that* any more.

MOONRAKING

Jackdaws and rooks usually seem to get along OK; you often see them flying or feeding in a mixed flock. But some kind of interesting fracas was going on overhead today with the rooks objecting to the jacks' presence, and I almost lost my footing watching them as I headed across the fields to the village. On the bus I relax and absorb the sights. Harrowing is taking place now under the autumn sun and blue sky with whitey-grey clouds. In Rousham (where else?) there's a sound I had forgotten, that of an old-fashioned push lawnmower. It speaks of sunny summers past, of Sundays when shops were closed, of small pleasures in small gardens, of men (it was usually men) occupied harmlessly. The women were indoors baking a cake for tea. It belongs with village cricket, and woodpigeons, and haunts of ancient peace. It has a scent, the scent of cut grass unmixed with the smell of petrol. Lawn mowing of any sort can seem a pretty pointless activity, but especially with an antiquated machine like this. Today it seems to be lived wisdom: slow, seasonal, persistent, traditional (the English and their shaved grass), creating a green matrix to set off the flowers, a place to sit quietly, a place to play. While that sound is occurring, Jeremy's Mum is lying in hospital, and people are getting blown up in Baghdad. It calls up those little windows of domesticity in *The Iliad* that so poignantly open in the walled blindness of war. It *needs* to be happening.

Through Steeple Aston, past the White Lion and the Red, past branches bent with plums, past a garden filled with a late summer glory made from little except small, self-seeded marigolds, and out onto the main road. The path opposite the Steeple Aston turn runs through a field that is at the moment ploughed, and I'm cheered to see that it's been reinstated. That's to say, a tractor has been driven up the line of it once or twice. It's a simple enough task, and one that the law requires, but that's often omitted either wilfully or neglectfully, and the effect is to discourage walkers. I am delighted to say that in Tackley parish the path up to the trig point and others, ones often planted over in the past, have been carefully marked out this spring. It's the good corollary of the tidiness that has cut down the standing but dead elms. Through Deddington, through Adderbury and Bodicote, signposts pointing off into the fields all the way — other days, other walks — but becoming increasingly built-up, until we finally make it through to Banbury Bus Station.

The Banbury town centre still teems with unregulated life, still harbours clutches of useful antibodies. It feels very different from Oxford. People on the street seem poorer, are more friendly. More of them seem to actually live there. It feels less like the south-east and more like the beginning of the midlands. Down its alleyways (urban footpaths) you can find odd small-budget shops and businesses — second-hand music, tacky drag or glad rags, birdseed, tattoos and piercings. The sort of places my mother (always paranoid and at one time O.D.ing on Conrad) was always convinced were 'a front' for something else. Certainly it's hard to see how some of them pay the rent, let alone make a profit. There are those who want it cleaned up to a seamless cloned glass-and-chromeness, where people out of old commercials (before they went postmodern) slide around its malls with brain-washed smiles and cash flow for blood. They're winning in places: the centre has the patchy appearance of a crown with alopecia. The latest loss is Hoods, the old-fashioned, well-stocked household shop which got surrounded by the clones but hung in there, like a good deed in a naughty world, apparently still thriving. Now suddenly it's gone, and being my mother's daughter I suspect foul play.

I am headed for the Tourist Information Centre to pick up (this will sound crazy) a leaflet about the circular walk in Deddington. I'd passed signs to this walk more than once, and sometimes discovered that I had actually walked parts of it. But I thought I should like to do the whole thing, and maybe find stuff out, about field-names, or a rare local beetle to look out for. The Post Office in Deddington said to try the Antique Shop. (How long ago was this walk created?) The Antique Shop had a notice specifically discouraging walkers in boots, but I nerved myself, leaned in at an angle, and asked very politely. They were right of course in thinking that amblers may muddy the carpet and almost certainly won't buy china, but that particular lady was friendly, and rifled helpfully through several boxes of printed ephemera, though without any luck. She suggested the Library, which was, of course, shut. I'm not a clever detective, being more like the plod from the Yard than Holmes or Poirot, but I do have the required persistence: I noted down the times and came back another day when they were open. No luck; nor at any of the shops I tried on the offchance. What I gleaned from all these questions and investigations was that there definitely *had been* leaflets, for the taking, but that no-one had seen one for quite a while. This was when it first (late in the day, but I've always been slow) dawned on me that the brief culture of genuine information and empowerment had vanished as quickly as it arose, seen off by the market, and targets, and lip service. People now exist to buy things rather than to do things or enjoy things.

I didn't realise this all at once. I negotiated my way through the maze of malls thinking I'd cracked it, that all I had to do was go in there, like a proper, modern tourist who understood that you needed to be centralised, and that I'd finally come out equipped. The Tourist Information Centre was palatial, and stocked with vast amounts of merchandise. Pricey merchandise. Packaged, a lot of it, as though it contained dangerous contaminants. The ladies were very busy, trading in biscuits, and fluffy toys, and embroidered bookmarks, so I didn't bother them to begin with, but wandered around the racks and bookshelves trying to find what I needed for myself. Finally in a lull I presented myself and my request, and was offered a pack of a dozen assorted leaflets in a rigid plastic pack which discouraged inspection prior to purchase and which retailed (I believe this is the term) at five pounds something. They said they were not supposed to sell them separately. I said they were not supposed to sell them at all, why weren't they free, and that most of the other places were too far north for me and off my bus route, and why weren't the Deddington ones available in Deddington? They riposted in the same way as Nathanael ('can there any good thing come out of Nazareth?'), the archetypal urban scorn of the provincial, the one-horse place. 'Where,' said one, as delivering the *coup de grâce*, 'where would we sell them in *Deddington*?'

Ironically, over the last few years Deddington has been rediscovering the true meaning of market. Every fourth Saturday it steps back in time and people who grow things, or keep livestock or make things, do business with the rest of us, and the rest of us stand in cheerful buzzing queues to get meat we've seen on the hoof and veg that is grown within walking distance and local apple juice. Like in France. At Christmas time they sell beakers of it hot and spiced and you stand around sipping and smiling and feeling good about life. Like in Germany, but more smiley because we're still so amazed at the sheer hands-on rightness of the thing. We asked about lemon thyme at a plant stall, and the stallholder said he would have some ready next month, and he did. We bought a new washing basket from a guy who sat on the ground plaiting them from willow. He looked as though he enjoyed what he was doing and was quietly proud of it. He said it should last a lifetime. He said he hoped it would serve us well. They serve you well too at The Unicorn, with breakfasts of local bacon and eggs and sausages and big thick hand-cut toast (not a pasty anorexic triangle in sight), and family parties hang out and girls haste about in versions of catering black, and the pinkest and busiest of all is wearing black cycling shorts. You almost expect them to call 'Anon, anon, sir' over their shoulders, like the hard-pressed drawers of Eastcheap in Shakespeare's *Henry IV*. On market days there is always music in the square, and like everything else there it is live.

I exit the Tourist Information Centre almost at a run, and the vapid mall, out onto the canal towpath where me and my boots belong. Walkers aren't tourists. They're sleuths and sometimes pilgrims. But the only intelligence I've picked up here is that Information is now a euphemism for marketing. And my spirit was starting to shrivel.

The water's a no-colour murk and totally opaque, like the water in the jam-jar when kids are painting. It perks up to khaki when the sun shines on it. Clean or dirty, it is water, and there is a path, and open air, and people doing something that costs nothing and gives them pleasure — strolling. We greet each other as we pass. One man gives me the Oxfordshire sideways nod that's on the way out. Young men don't do it, and I don't think women ever did. It feels like a benediction. My eyes feast — so starved they have been — on the mallard-green sheen of the flies on a pile of dogshit. You still have to run the gauntlet, before you can quite make good your escape; from one bank come the powerful and noxious fumes of paint from some kind of works, and from the other the stench of burning rubber. Your body instinctively knows this is bad for it, and every cell yells *Scarper, get the hell out!* It is pitiful to think of the circumscription of imagination and life-choice that can induce people to work there. How come it's legal? I get through the worst of it and then, against my body's advice, pick a handful of squishy, large-lobed, and undoubtedly toxic blackberries, with the confused idea that it somehow supports the resistance.

The carcass of a narrow-boat has fetched up on the bank and become a little wooden shop. MOONRAKER, 65FT. No-one seems to be around to take your money, but someone has grown thyme and sage and chives in flowerpots which they've painted with the traditional canal motifs and set out for sale. Somehow you know they haven't set their sights on a chain of garden centres. Live boats go slowly by carrying people in a trance of quiet delight. A man raises his glass to me. A lone woman, steering very carefully, says, 'They said it would rain today, we're lucky…' Oh, we are. We've had a narrow escape so far from becoming counters in the plastic utopia; but it's spreading out. It means to net us all. Cucumbers are growing in a rack beside a mooring; ('Fourteen days without charge', a notice says.) Real cool, man. Signifying life and hope and doing your own green thing. To my utter astonishment, a fish leaps. My heart too.

It's still townish, with a town park on the west bank, with grass and litter and litter bins and benches and non-native trees, but I soon stop crunching and am walking quietly on beaten earth, and on this bank through an old laid hawthorn hedge, punctuated by big oaks that have dropped their acorns underfoot, you can glimpse pasture. Elderberries are ripe, earlier than usual. Nettles and meadowsweet begin to encroach on the path as the foot traffic dwindles. There are clumps of butterbur with its big rhubarb-like leaves, beginning to go rusty, and pretty stands of orange balsam and dry heads of umbels that are beautiful but autumnal. Nevertheless it's hot enough for sweating and enjoying breeze on the back of the neck and the pleasant change when trees overhang. Soon you can see and hear the motorway, with its metallic infestation shiny as the greenbottles in the sun. Here on the path, there's a huge brown dragonfly and a small orange butterfly with scalloped wings. A comma, I learn that evening, whose second brood flies in late August. Is flying now, in other words, just as it should. That was once found only in the Wye Valley, but has spread widely. *Floreat Polygonia C-Album*!

On a lonely stretch I pass two beaten-in boats which don't look as though they could move any longer even if they wanted to, but do seem to be tenuously inhabited. A Heath Robinson barbecue is set up in mid-path: they obviously don't get many passers-by. A stripy dragonfly, a speckled brown butterfly, and several whites. Mallows, and a plant scent I can't place, a mixture of pepper and sweetness. On the further bank the spirit of Bevis lives on, undefeated by the virtual — two boys are playing at being boys from the past, fooling around by the swing bridge, dipping sticks, melting puckishly into the vegetation at my approach. Further along, on my side, a surreally large blue-grey teddy bear and a child's rusting bike have oddly been abandoned in the hedge. Autumn insists again that it has arrived, with thirty or so young brown starlings hunched on a wire, and rooks and pigeons feeding in the stubble. I expected Twyford Wharf to be all ropes and coals and chandlers' shops, but I was disappointed. There was some kind of very tidy enterprise with no living person visible, called the Twilite Leisure Park. I hurry past nervously in case they see me on their monitors and reel me in, like in *The Prisoner*.

I decide to take in Bodicote, and find three shut pubs. More and more I begin to appreciate The Carpenter's Arms in Middle Barton, quietly open mid-afternoon mid-week and not on a main road. And the friendly White Lion in Steeple Aston where they welcomed me one afternoon soaked almost to the waist where I'd waded through flooded meadows, gave me tea, with a homemade biscuit, and a fireside, and begged me not to bother to take my boots off unless I wished to myself. But in Bodicote at least the church is open and I sit inside its coolness for a while, enjoying the gingery scent of the pink lilies and reading the board which advertises an organisation called LOAF, promoting local organic food. When I pass the Methodists, they too are stretching out to a non-religious good cause: they have a poster for Roadpeace.

I wander along the village streets enjoying the glimpses of gardens. There is pink phlox, and there are blue geraniums. And lemon balm: I nip off a small piece to press and sniff as I walk along. It's the sort of day when doors stand open and you can sometimes see right through to the back. Warm weather opens things up. Places are like poetry, I'm beginning to realise, and can be open or closed, and I don't just mean their shops or pubs or churches, but the whole feel of them. The poets I love are the ones who let you in, not the ones who have made a hard, walled-in structure for you to admire. That really is another book I guess; but I love footpaths because of what they open up.

There's a Greek song I used to play a lot called 'Anthi tes petras' — flowers from the stones, and I once knew a guy who was in a band called Stoneflower. There's something poignant and appealing about the juxtaposition of plant and stone. I watch every year for my friends' Doug and Judy's tall hollyhocks in the Nethercote Road in Tackley, which seem almost an outgrowth of their low stone cottage, and there are some here in Bodicote. I am taken too by the wood sorrel, tenderest of weeds, growing out of the very base of a house with no soil visible at all. Smells drift out — an old-fashioned cabbagy dinner smell, a hot synthetic hairdressing smell. And sounds: a tranny where there are decorators working, the wing-clap of a wood pigeon from a big garden tree.

A very old lady takes a long time getting off the bus, with her two sticks, and I feel very fortunate suddenly, and resolve not to take my legs for granted.

My evening's rooting which identified the comma, with its curious and lovely wings cut out like the leaves of white bryony, also unearthed Moonraker, a sub-species of homo sapiens. I never had known what it meant. Apparently it has been used to mean a native of Wiltshire, from a story that some locals were trying to catch the moon's reflection in a pond. They defended themselves against the slur of daftness by saying they were actually recovering their contraband liquor, but needed to fool the excisemen. In other words, it was 'a front'. So there's an appealing combination of daft and crafty there. It has a nautical meaning too, the highest sail, even above the sky sail; but that wouldn't be narrowboat-speak. The Shorter O.E.D., under Moonraking, *fig.* has the word 'woolgathering' which the smallprint big dic, the one with the magnifying glass, for some reason omits. I'll drink to that. Gleaning, woolgathering, moonraking. As healthy pursuits for the mind as ambling is for the body, and they all go together.

WHERE TO?

The flooded fields lay silver under a sky of grey cloud, the south-westerly breeze making them appear to be flowing. The cattle were all lying down on the higher ground of the deserted village. The way to Pigeons Lock was impassable, waist-deep at least. Many of the minor paths were overgrown or at least overhung with nettles and tall sopping grasses and wild flowers. It seemed like a day to do a stretch of the Oxfordshire Way. A long-distance path crossing the county from Henley to Bourton-on-the-Water, the section from here to Stonesfield follows the line of a Roman road, Akeman Street. When the trail was first created there were obstructions and problems over the route, even though it used existing rights of way. Now that it's well-established you can be fairly confident of being able to get along without struggling through crops or getting lost. It runs right by our house — 'Field Cottage, Old Whitehill' features in the official walker's guide as a landmark, and for some reason that pleases me. It speaks of permanence. I don't know how they got the name because it is nowhere displayed, but I'm glad they did.

I start off along the lane and up the hill, and join the Way at the telephone hut. My neighbours have done some tree planting over the years, and a young lime they put in is now in full flower and fragrance. Lime is one of the best gifts of July — a free and ubiquitous aromatherapy treatment. The tall and slightly alien pines along their driveway are sounding of the sea, as they always do in any breeze or wind, bringing a touch of wildness to our lives. The plantation on Pound Hill is really a wood now, and the larches in it are laden with cones and have lively yellow-green growing tips. Opposite the post-box, where the lane meets another, is a small grassy plat which must be at its blossoming best — a subtle blend of mauves and yellows and white. I can identify scabious, yellow vetchling and lady's bedstraw, and a dainty, small-flowered white campion. Akeman Street is ahead at right-angles, intersecting with the lane. Several of the dead elms along it have come down now, but some, ivy-covered, are still standing among a mix of other tall deciduous trees. The rookery has upped sticks since the Dutch elm disease came, but the remaining trees are still used for mass rallies of corvines when something has raised them from feeding on the Dairy Ground below. Today rooks and jacks are in two camps on two different trees, all calling in that rackety and troubled way they seem to in breezy weather.

The laneside hedge, a mixed planting a few years old, looks to be thriving. Countryside legislation is a Polly and Suky affair. Last year a 'bumble-bee patch' was planted in the set-aside field beside the house. Darren was quick to throw down the notice explaining about it of course, but the richer flora was looking and smelling lovely, and the bees obviously thought so too. This year bulldozers have hacked it all down to lay a new pipeline. In the past few years there's been replanting of hedges ripped out in the '70s and '80s, often with mixed native species. Among the basic hawthorn may be maple, hazel, dogwood... even the occasional witchy spindleberry with its interestingly-shaped, shocking pink poisonous berries. The rule of thumb for dating hedges — one species per hundred years — goes out of the window, but who cares? The resulting hedges are variously beautiful, and an encouragement to a variety of bird and insect species. In the same way, unsown arable margins are starting to bring back some wild flowers to our fields, and some of the ground-nesting birds. So maybe now we can all have tea.

Here beside the Oxfordshire Way between its grassy surface and the drying rape is a band of tall weeds, the predominant one being one of those yellow *compositae* — sow-thistle? Whatever it is, small birds love it — either the seeds or the insects that live on the plants. Numbers of tits and finches fly out and into the band of woodland on my right, as I pass along. And from the wood I can hear a repeated call I can't place. I resolve to revisit this birdy stretch soon, with binoculars. Two swallows swoop low over the crop. White bedstraw stretches up dainty but tall against the bottom of the hedge. Through an arched gap in the thorn there is a classic vista of golden wheat with dark green trees on the far side, reminding me how relatively recent a crop is the oilseed rape on my left. I swish along softly over the mown grass, wishing I didn't hear the occasional crunch as I crush a small snail.

Emerging onto the road at the Tackley turn someone smiles at me from a car. It's not someone I recognise; the smile is for a walker, for someone out doing a truly recreational thing. When such smiles come my way they tell me that we all at heart want simple, natural, free and innocent pleasures. And that we love the earth. Waving at trains is the same sort of thing. Originally, I imagine, people waved excitedly, saying 'Look at you in that amazing conveyance!' and the train travellers (they were not customers then) would wave back in acknowledgment of the adventure, and of their astonishing, exotic status. Those who still keep up the custom — and I am one of them whether out or in — are saying something slightly different, something more fundamental. Something like, 'I greet you, fellow earth-dweller. I'm one with you, even though I live here and you flash by; even though I flash by and you live here. I too walk/take the train sometimes, and I know its pleasures. Life has different speeds at different times. Good luck!'

Eventually I get a break and cross the fast main road, entering a tree tunnel with a floor of soft sandy earth, full of holes. Rabbits live here I should say Holmes, and at least one eater of Maltesers has passed this way. The big roadhouse is called Sturdy's Castle, carrying in its name a memory of highwaymen and turnpikes. The next one north used to be Hopcroft's Holt: Hopcroft was another. It's now gone upmarket as the Holt Hotel. There's a smell of wood-smoke, and though a gap I can see a couple of blokes leaning on forks and watching a blaze they have made. The path soon crosses Slough Lane, an old green way. The book writes it thus — Slough — and certainly it is often miry, especially when horseriders have been along it; but I've never been convinced that it isn't actually Sloe Lane, because it's the best place around to come if you're going to have a go at one of the most surefire of Richard Mabey's *Food for Free* ideas — sloe gin. Slough or Sloe, my path is a drier one, closed with a new wooden hunting gate since I last came this way, but one that opens easily onto the grassy, flowery balk that leads to Sansom's Plat, where Roman bits and pieces have been found. Here the fields on either hand are planted with wheat, but with two wide swathes of arable margin. There are cheerful pink mallows, and the occasional accent of a poppy. By now small windows of blue have opened in the cloud. A single swift wheels over the wheat, and more soon follow. Yellowhammers sing their rattly songs.

Now the path is neatly hedged with hogweed, almost as though it were planted, and another new gate lets you out onto Dornford Lane, another old green lane, though recently turned into more of a yellow lane, having been surfaced by Sustrans so that cycles can use it. Paths, even ancient ones, don't carry the same clout as old buildings. If you'd proposed to pebble-dash Blenheim Palace there'd be an outcry. For my ex-farm cottage to have a lean-to for logs I had to apply to the Historical Monuments Commission. I can't deny that the Sustrans surface makes easier going for walkers too — in fact it seems to be mainly walkers whom it benefits because a cyclist is a rare sight. But something has been lost. If private cars were to be done away with and we all went by foot and horse and cycle then the main road, with its often pointless journeys and noise and fumes and entirely avoidable injuries and deaths, would become transformed and could be used by all… It's pleasant to dream. As things are, a kind of suburbanness is encroaching all the time, tidying, licking our countryside into shape and in the process, as the painter Graham Arnold once memorably said to me, it is driving the small gods out.

A lone cottage has been 'done up' but to my eyes is wretchedly transformed. From the faux-Gothic sign to the quick-growing spruces it seems not to belong in the countryside any more. It used to have a simple and colourful cottage garden, sunflowers and roses and bean rows and spuds, one of those gardens that feed the spirit as you walk by them. Now you can see into it only from a distance and all that's visible is a heap of what looks like large packaging. From close to you can see nothing over the high forbidding fences that have been put in place; and where once you could exchange a quiet greeting and a word of admiration with the gardener, there is now both CCTV and guard dogs to let you know that you are most unwelcome.

And the path itself now actually takes to the tarmac for half a mile or so. A surprising number of cars use this stretch too, as a cut-through. One would think that a footpath to one side is the least that could be done, but footpaths don't come high on the recreation budget. Pressing close to the hedge you pass along as quick as you can, although kingfisher and moorhen sound at the crossing of the Glyme. Up again out of the valley beneath the softly terracotta keys of leaves of the field maples and the green drapes of bryony which will turn into old man's beard. A baby rabbit has been glued to the road. Roads are for the dead and paths for the living. In a car one is cut off from all the delightful minutiae of what Edmund Blunden called the 'sounds and scents and seeings' that infuse us with joy in life. Where the minor road meets the main road is a fine stand of mullein, tall woolly glaucous-leaved spires of yellow flowers. There's something defiant about them, like the buddleias in a scrapyard. A woman friend was being ordained as a priest, and another friend bought her, instead of a spiritual book or whatever, a posh red satin slip to wear under her vestments. On hearing what it was for, the lady in shop wrapped it reflectively in tissue. 'It…sort of…gives one hope, doesn't it?' she said as she handed it over.

Again I take my life in my hands to cross to Wootton Door. The gate into the first defensive ring surrounding Blenheim Park drops down on its hinge and is hard to put back up — quite surprising on a major walking route because it suggests not a great deal of use — and the path itself is a little overgrown. The inner ring is a high stone wall with the big wooden door set into it, which opens on a narrow belt of trees, and then you are soon out into a yellow and purple meadow of thistles and Oxford ragwort and a myriad small hawkbits. There are patches of a low-growing plant with small fat purple flowerheads, that I think may be self-heal, and there are one or two bees on them and on the sweet white clover. Only this morning I heard on the news that bees are in trouble, and so now I'm noticing them, and how sparse they seem. Something else that we can't take for granted. By the gate into a small farmyard is a single perfect pyramidal orchid.

There's a small newish plantation of oaks and chestnuts, but the buildings themselves seem to be derelict. Yet it looks like a good place to live, and faceless houses are going up by main roads everywhere. Someone did live here when the Oxfordshire Way was first devised, a farmer who didn't like the idea of it at all, and used to run his bull on the path until Rowland Pomfret sorted things out. Rowland, who I was proud to call a friend, did more for the paths of West Oxfordshire than anyone before or since. He once had me sit on the runway at Kidlington Airport with him until the police were called, to draw attention to the need to sort out the right of way. Rowland never reached retirement age. He worked full-time, and all his astonishing load of footpath work was done in evenings and at weekends. His enthusiasm and tenacity were unparalleled. He left us a legacy that is better than money or things: every step we take in this part of the country is in his footsteps and very often directly thanks to his fight to have signs put up, stiles and bridges restored, barbed wire taken down and paths left unplanted. There must be footpaths in heaven, or Rowland would never be happy there.

A small group of sheep and lambs run blunderingly ahead of me, making me their unwilling herdswoman, until one of them has the sense to lollop off to one side, and the rest follow. A lark rises singing. There's now a wide grassy track with a metalling of stones showing through and a border of pink-flowered lesser bindweed. The double avenue of small prim limes crosses like a crocodile of kids, to my eye less attractive than the taller variety. I prefer the one or two taller skirted clumps of trees set in the grass – the classic parkland landscape. The angry, busy noise of a power saw sounds from a nearby copse. One or two native hedge trees have been planted, but a spindleberry leans awkwardly sideways out of its wire sheath as though trying to escape. And then the green path itself suddenly morphs into a hard-surfaced white roadway with electric fences either side, and beyond them untenanted, uninteresting, single-species grassland without a single wild flower. The complete effectiveness of the weed-killing job is depressing, and the few tiny scarlet pimpernels and blue bird's-eyes by the gate seem suddenly very precious. Beyond the gate is a narrow belt of trees and then here is the park wall again. The ladder stile over it, which is known as Stonesfield Steps, is very like the one in Millais' picture *Waiting*, on which a cloaked and bonneted young woman sits pensively, waiting, presumably, for her lover. The wide flat top of it seems a good place for lunch, so I sit and enjoy it, and the sun, which is coming out more all the time, and rest my eyes on the pleasantly varied landscape ahead, and the first distant roofs of the village.

An estate that in its time has produced salted venison, fish, eels, pork, reed, eggs, rabbits, hops and honey and more, seems poor now with its big shows and vapid giftshop and artificial kids' amusements that leave no residue in the spirit. Yesterday a little girl on the bus had been to Blenheim on a school trip. 'What did you see?' her mother asked. 'Nothing.' I sympathised, even though she was being cussed. I am feeling freed. 'Something there is,' as Robert Frost wrote, 'that doesn't love a wall. That wants it down.'

There is more life out here, so it feels, in every sense. The land looks more fertile. There is wheat on either side of the path, and whitish nuts in the hedge. And what is that whitish whole field ahead. Could it be potatoes? Spuds indeed they prove to be, in two varieties, one with denser and pinker flowers. There's a machine with a huge hose coiled on it, presumably for irrigation. There are more wild flowers out here, and more butterflies: whitey green butterflies, scabious, knapweed, meadow browns, a small tortoiseshell. The very slope of the land is more interesting. The path is warmly sheltered by the hedge and scented with bedstraw. To one side is now a field of red-gold barley.

The new yellow houses on the outskirts of Stonesfield are brash but will mellow. At least they have chimneys. A house with no hearth has no heart. I once endured a year in Washington D.C. without a hearth and no amount of central heating kept the spiritual chill at bay. The young bin men, two white and one black, are sorting the recycling by hand. I hope it's enough and in time. I call in briefly on my friend Val who has been *thoroughly* enjoying her new grandchild, and view the baby photos and then catch the bus to Oxford. A really great website *travelinesouth-east* makes you realise that many destinations are possible, with cheerful little pictures of buses and trains and feet, and because of this I've begun to use North Oxford as a hub (I don't need to tangle with the city) and reach for more places with my bus pass. In Oxford there is time before the bus, so I call on my friend Diana, who is out. But her partner Heathcote Williams, who wrote that wonderful indictment of cars *Autogeddon*, gives me tea and tiffin. He's perfecting the recipe: for this version he has soaked the raisins in brandy... I manage to stop after two pieces and go to catch the bus home, with a piece of thyme from their front step stuck in my buttonhole. Another friend's son, Igor, passes by as I wait for the bus, a young man who has something rare and infectious in his zest for life. We congratulate each other on having equally uncool but practical sunhats. If I'd gone out in the car, chances are as well as missing out on the nature I wouldn't have seen any of these friends who have cheered my day.

Walking home from the Green, where the bus drops me, I revel in Tackley itself. It's all I can do not to praise it aloud, with its brilliant trend-bucking shop run with the help of a volunteer rota and its warm-hearted school that made my globe-trotting grandchildren so welcome for a term. The curved metal kissing-gates rusted to a beech-nut brown squeak and clang familiarly as they admit me. The sheep belt away as usual across the small in-by pasture. The old chestnut in the corner, by the next gate, is covered in the prickly green-cased fruit. A woodpigeon is gentling the afternoon. A pinkish umbel-flower is covered in red flying beetle-type things — and one bee. The very lichen circles on the park wall have a soft and friendly look. The smell of the lime blossom seems to nourish some part of me. Peter's Spout Ground is muddy and warm and full of butterflies and insects. Darren seems to have had a go at the bridge but you can still get across. (A few weeks later it's been mended, and reinforced.) The set-aside flutters with marbled whites and feathery grasses. Two swallows and an ancient-looking brown dragon overfly it. The air is full of ticking and twittering. On the homeward lap two dogs are coming towards me, but they don't bark.